THE HIDDEN STREAM

RONALD A. KNOX

The Hidden Stream

IGNATIUS PRESS   SAN FRANCISCO

Cover by Christopher J. Pelicano

Reprinted 2003 Ignatius Press, San Francisco
ISBN 0-89870-863-x
Library of Congress Control Number 2002105234
Printed in the United States of America (∞)

CONTENTS

PREFACE

It is ten years now since I published *In Soft Garments*, a selection of the conferences I had given to the Catholic undergraduates at Oxford while I was their chaplain. The same course of apologetics still goes on; and, since my resignation, the kindness of my successors has made a point of my coming back, once every term, to take part in it. The result is that my store of back-numbers is full to bursting again, and calls for a fresh salvage-drive. Here, then, is a new set of conferences, which inevitably covers the same sort of ground, or even the same ground, as the old; where fundamentals of the faith are concerned, a fresh generation of undergraduates is exercised by the same problems as the last. But the treatment, in these new essays, is different—whether for better or worse, it is not for me to say; I only know that, for the most part, they were more laboriously written.

It remains to give some explanation of the title I have chosen. The lane which runs past the Old Palace (where these conferences were delivered) bears every mark of being a closed-in water-course, and so indeed it is; here the Trill Mill Stream, a true branch of Isis that has flowed modestly through the less frequented parts of Oxford, goes underground for a few hundred yards, to issue under an ornamental bridge in the Christ Church Memorial Garden. If you know the right turning, close by the gas-works, you may thrust your canoe up to the mill-pool under the Castle walls, where an entrance hardly more dignified than that of a sewer invites you to leave the noise of Oxford behind, and float down through the darkness.

Five centuries ago, before the mill-stream was covered in, it must have hurried past the walls of the Franciscan, then of

7

the Dominican friary, accepting its tribute of grey cowls and black competitively washed. Those rivalries have vanished; invisible, now, it burrows its way under the discreet postern of Campion Hall, the pious uproar of the Old Palace. But it is the same channel, and a true water-course; not all of Isis flows under Folly Bridge or meanders about the shoals of the Seacourt Stream. And (if I must drag my parable to the light) not all the philosophies of Oxford are philosophies of negation and despair; she is fed by secret streams, not less influential to her life or less native to her genius.

[1953]

What Is Religion?

Stevenson, I think in *Virginibus Puerisque*, has preserved for us a letter written to a man by his aunt, on the subject of a young lady who would, she thought, be a good person for this nephew of hers to marry. And she goes through a list of the various talents and accomplishments the young lady has, mentioning among others, "about as much religion as my William likes". I think in any discussion of religion it is important to rule out *that* idea of it from the first. It is not a kind of accomplishment, like painting on china, of which it is important that the *débutante* should have a smattering so as to increase her value in the matrimonial market. It is fair to mention that I think "my William" is a rather common figure in the non-Catholic world; he rather prefers it if the girl he wants to marry is mildly religious in that sort of way; and it is our fault if we let that idea of what religion means become current. It is because we practise religion in a rather languid, external way that people get the impression it is a sort of bloom on the surface of our lives which makes us more attractive people; a sort of added grace of character which some people have, some haven't. Whatever else it is—let us be clear about that from the outset—religion is something we belong to, not something which belongs to us; something that has got hold of us, not something we have got hold of. It is something which determines our whole approach and our whole relation to life; if it is not that, if it is to be a mere fad or a mere pose, it had better be cut out altogether.

That you can see even from its derivation. I don't think there can be any real doubt that it is derived from the Latin verb *religare*, to bind, to tie down. I don't apologize for inflicting Latin verbs on you, because in a curious way you can say that religion is both a Latin word and a Latin thing, whereas theology is a Greek word and a Greek thing. The Greeks liked to talk about the gods, bring them into speeches and lend a tone to literature with them, but they didn't like *doing* anything about them; they lived by their philosophy, if they lived by any rule at all. Whereas the Romans, till they began to go Greek, were for ever worrying about taboos and ceremonies and omens; they lived a life haunted by the unseen, and they were always trying to dodge the implications of it. Above all, religion meant that if you swore an oath you had got to keep it; it bound you. That predominating sense has survived in modern ecclesiastical language. When we talk about monks or nuns as "religious" what we are saying is not that they are holier people than ourselves, though no doubt they usually are holier people than ourselves. What we are saying is that they are bound by vows, and we are not. They can't go out and get drunk even if they want to.

When we have said that, we have said enough to make ourselves feel that religion is a rather unpleasant thing. In the first place because it seems to be no better, at least in its origins, than a kind of magic. And in the second place because it is something merely negative; it is a drag upon one's life, not an inspiration to live by. Let us take those two objections in that order.

I think I am right in saying that it is bad anthropology to regard magic as the ancestor of religion. It would be truer to say that magic is the ancestor of science. The medical man of to-day comes down to us from the medicine man of centuries ago; but the centuries have been centuries of trial and error, so he knows his stuff better. The business of the scientist, as of the magician, is first to discover the causes of things and then to avoid their effects. He is trying to exploit man's surroundings in the interests of man. But religion, you see, is just the other way up; its object, if you can put the thing as crudely as that, is to exploit man in the interest of his surroundings. The magician tries to see how much he can get out of God for man; the priest tries to see how much he can get out of man for God. Of course, in any primitive society the two things are always getting mixed up, and it isn't easy to say where religion begins and magic ends. In setting out to make amends to the god you have somehow offended, you are also trying to get rid of the drought or the cholera which he has sent to punish you. But in idea the two things are separate.

And not only are they separate in idea, but they develop as time goes on in opposite directions. Magic thins out into scientific research; tabooism thins out into a religion of personal holiness. One pedigree ends in Rutherford, the other in Gandhi. Science gets more and more externalized; drops the spells and the incantations, sticks to the lancet and the pills. Religion gets more and more internalized, comes to regard the action of worshipping the image as less important than the attitude of the worshipper towards his god, the lustral water as less important than purity of life.

I have been talking so far of unrevealed, and therefore of false, religions; but those of you who know anything about the Old Testament will realize that much of what I have been saying goes, also, for the partial revelation which Almighty God made to the Jews. The chief mission and the chief difficulty of the Jewish prophets was to persuade their fellow-countrymen that it wasn't much good trying to appease God with the blood of bulls and goats if you went on bearing false witness and oppressing the poor at the same time. Religion wasn't meant to tie you down from touching a dead body or seething a kid in its mother's milk. It was meant to tie you down to a rule of right living, a rule of love towards God and towards your fellow man.

And now we have to consider the other objection, that

religion is by its very definition, and therefore in its very
nature, a purely negative thing, always telling you *not* to do
something, never telling you *to* do something. All these taboos which you find in the old Roman religion, and also in
most savage religions, are not, after all, the stuff of which
they are made. One can imagine some primitive set of people
who were bound by a whole code of regulations as negative
and as meaningless as the instinct which makes some people
always want to walk on the paving-stones, never setting foot
on the cracks between the paving-stones. But as a matter of
fact you don't find that. The whole point of religion is to
believe in the existence of some power or powers behind the
scenes, and believe that it is important for you to keep on the
right side of them. They haunt a particular spot; there is, as
the Romans would have said, a *religio loci*; it is up to you to
avoid that spot, because it would be blundering in on a set of
powers who are too big for you; and you do avoid it, just as
you would avoid the cracks between the paving-stones if you
thought that some deity inhabited the cracks between the
paving-stones. There is a particular day of the month which
is for some reason held sacred to one of those powers; and it
may be you observe that day in a negative way—say, by not
going out to battle; but once more the prohibition implies
something positive; you don't unaccountably avoid that day
in the first instance and invent a deity afterwards to account
for your reluctance. No, you have the feeling that you are
hedged about by majestic presences belonging to another
world than this world which you see, and the nearer you
come in contact with them, the more you have to be on your
good behaviour; that is all. If you do go near the sacred spot,
you must somehow mark the difference by your own
behaviour; you must take your shoes off, for example. Not
wearing your shoes is something negative; and so natural is it
to mark the difference by *not* doing something, that you are
led to describe your attitude towards these powers as an attitude of negation; it is a *religio*, something which restrains you.

But your *reason* is not a negative one, it is a positive one; you feel you are not alone—there is Somebody just behind that tree.

How far this feeling of the uncanny, this sense that certain places, for example, are haunted by supernatural presences, can be used to prove the truth of religion, I don't know. It is fashionable, I believe, to argue that this sense of awe, this sense of the "numinous", is a thing which could not be explained if there were not something real behind it. I am never very fond of that kind of argument myself. But I do think you can say this; that if mankind generally, for thousands of years, has been in the habit of recognizing, and living up to, the presence of an unseen spiritual world, it is likely that this attitude of worship is part of man's natural make-up. He is the only animal that finds it comfortable to remain on bent knees. *Dis te minorem quod geris, imperas*; if we are lords of creation, it is only as the vassals of an Overlord higher than ourselves—if it were not so, how could we be so ludicrously incomplete, so undignified, so dissatisfied as we are? Say, if you like, that our habit of addressing worship to Powers whom we think of as reigning above us is an inference, perhaps an unconscious inference, from that feeling of inferiority. Say, if you will, that it is an instinct, which neither has nor demands an explanation, apart from the obvious explanation that a supernatural world really exists, containing Powers that are worthy of worship. What seems evident in either case is that we are built to be a half-way house between the natural and the supernatural; that adoration is a congenital posture with us. If we try to rise above our own level we immediately sink beneath our own level, for we lose our place in creation.

And that is, to my mind, I won't say the most important answer, but the most interesting answer to the next question that comes up to be considered. The question, I mean, "What is the advantage of having a religion, as opposed to having none?" There are all sorts of answers, obviously, that can be given. You can treat it as a mere question of happiness; point out how much fuller life is if you believe that Man has a tangible end to fulfil, and is doing so under the eyes of a benign Task-master—still more if you believe, as our religion teaches and many others teach, that there will be a reward for us, in another world, if the task is well done. You can treat it as a question of intellectual satisfaction; point out that all the riddles which our thought comes up against, as it tries this avenue of speculation or that, become less of a nightmare to us if we believe that there is a supreme Intelligence which knows the answer to them all, even where it is hidden from us. You can treat it as a question of general human well-being: how long would it be before we threw over all the restraints of morality, if we did not believe that there were supernatural sanctions at the back of all our ideas of right and wrong? Oh, to be sure, we all know good atheists. But we all have the feeling about them that they are, as it were, chewing the cud of that Christianity in which their ancestors believed; they are living up to a code which is in fact Christian, although they do not acknowledge it. Construct a godless civilization and you do not have to wait long before you find out whether the children bred in it acquire pretty habits or not. All that is true; that the world would be very much poorer if it had no leaven of religion in it, and that a great many of us, who haven't got good digestions to start with, would find life a pretty poor show if there were no elements in the make-up of it besides those which we meet with in the daily experience of our senses.

But, as I say, I think the most interesting answer to the question, "What difference does religion make?" is just to point at the people who haven't got any, and leave it to be solved by inspection. I don't mean the happy-go-lucky people who don't seem to bother about religion or anything else much; they can be quite good company. But your profession-ally irreligious person, if I may use that phrase, is such a bad advertisement, I think, for his absence of religion. I don't

want to put a name to it, to describe their atmosphere as one
of bumptiousness, or as one of priggishness, or as one of
shocking bad manners; I would prefer to say that there is
something definitely subhuman about it; there's a blind spot
in them which makes all human commerce with them
difficult, which makes the room seem more comfortable
when they have gone out of it. But that may be only a
personal fad of mine, so I won't go on about it.

But no, there's a very important point to be raised which
we haven't raised yet. Granted that religion is all we say, that
it makes people happier, makes them less bewildered, makes
them better citizens, makes them (if I am any judge of the
matter) more comfortable people to meet—is it necessary
that the religion one holds should be true? Or will a bogus
one do? You see, we have been treating religion, after all, as if
it were a mere attitude one can adopt towards life, and as we
think a worthwhile attitude. But surely it would be equally
effective if, as a matter of fact, there were no supernatural
realities behind it. The peace of Europe can be preserved as
long as *this* country thinks *that* country has a secret weapon
capable of finishing any war in forty-five minutes; the existence of the weapon doesn't matter as long as it is *thought* to
be there. The question, I need hardly say, is not often raised
in that form. But it is often raised in the subsidiary form,
"Does it matter what a man believes, or how much he believes, as long as it gives him that religious attitude towards
life which, everybody agrees, is so valuable?"

You meet that doubt in any number of forms; people
telling you that one kind of Christianity is as valuable as
another, as long as it makes people good and happy, and
therefore we Catholics oughtn't to proselytize. Public men
getting up and telling us that England is finished unless we
can introduce some religion into the Youth Movement, without saying what religion. People like Aldous Huxley making
out that mysticism is the only thing which is worth having,
and whether it is Christian or Buddhist mysticism is only a

matter of detail. People like his brother wondering if we couldn't make do with a kind of synthetic religion—"emotion tinged with morality", the Victorians used to call it—based not on any belief in the supernatural world but on a conspiracy to behave as if the supernatural world was there. All *that* happens, you see, the moment you start going about saying that religion is a good thing. You are understood, not unreasonably, to mean that the religious *attitude* is a good thing. Is religion just that, or something more? Where does the *Credo* come into it?

The truth is that the word "religion" under the Christian dispensation has changed its meaning. It does not stand for a mere attitude, it stands for a transaction; if you will, for the paying off of a debt. Religion, in our sense, means the offering up of a man's self to God; for us Christians, it means the offering up to God of Jesus Christ, the perfect Victim once for all immolated in our stead, and of ourselves in union with that sacrifice. It means an adoration which aims, if that were possible, at annihilating our own creaturely existence so as to give God the honour which is his due. Religion in our sense is a claim; the claim which God has upon us for worship of whatever kind, and in whatever currency, he demands. The Jews under the old dispensation were not making a foolish mistake in offering up bulls and rams, however primitive, mechanical and messy that kind of sacrifice may seem to us. They were doing what he told them to do, acknowledging their creatureliness and mystically immolating it to him by taking the life of dumb creatures. He has done us a greater honour; he demands of us, more explicitly and more stringently than of them, that we should offer up ourselves, souls and bodies, as a reasonable sacrifice; that is, a human sacrifice, not one of brute beasts. Religion is adoring God.

Incidentally, it does claim from us a conditioning of our behaviour; we are to live the Christ-imitating life. That demand still ties us down; or shall we rather say that it ties us up? That is integrates us, makes of our souls a unity, in which reason governs the other faculties, and reason itself is subject to God? But equally, religion claims from us the adherence of our intellect to truths which God has revealed; a Christ-imitating life which still denies him the homage of believing what he tells us is a life imperfectly Christian. Don't let us sit down, then, under descriptions of "religion" or "Christianity" which imply that it is simply a dodge to keep you straight at school. The world around us is all too ready to talk in that way, and to rejoice if we allow it to be assumed that we agree with the description. God knows we have to be careful, in a censorious society, not to let it be said that we Catholics don't bother much about the moral, or the civic, virtues. But don't let us imagine that any code of conduct, keeping our word, or controlling our senses, or being kind towards our neighbours, is itself the Christian thing. It is only the flower springing from the root; and the root is humbling ourselves, offering ourselves, annihilating ourselves, in the presence of Almighty God.

2

Does Proof Matter?

I am not considering, here, whether the classical proofs of the existence of God do or do not hold water. I am only asking the question: What effective value have these proofs for the minds of ordinary men and women to-day? What changes have come over our world-outlook since the schoolmen enunciated them, and to what extent have those changes immunized our minds against the appeal which such ways of thinking had for our forefathers? After all, an argument may be perfectly water-tight when you consider it in the abstract, and yet fail to produce a practical conviction in the minds of living men and women. They may say, "Yes, I confess I don't see any way of getting round your arguments; but they don't, somehow, make me want to do anything about it." And that is, perhaps, more discouraging than the most determined opposition which the philosopher can encounter.

Imagine yourself a Dominican friar in Oxford five hundred years ago, studying and commenting on St Thomas's five proofs, a hundred yards or so from where we are sitting now. Think what a nice compact world he lives in. Geographically compact; he lives on the outskirts of a world which is still, for practical purposes, centred round a Mediterranean lake. It is peopled by Catholics—you must remember that, at this time, the schism between East and West appeared to have been patched up—by a handful of unimportant heretics, the Jews, and a dark background of terrible Mahommedans, who are, nevertheless, good monotheists.

Atheism is only a freak notion, cultivated by a few learned men; idolaters are people you have read about in books, dead now and in hell. A world, too, intellectually compact; science, philosophy, and theology are not three disparate branches of learning, but three rungs in a single educational ladder. From the contemplation of nature you rise to pure thought; from pure thought, grace elevates you to the contemplation of the supernatural. You are an extrovert; your mind is not given to continual returns upon itself, such as might breed misgivings about your own processes of thought, or the reality of the world you live in. You can indulge in a hundred odd and apparently unorthodox speculations, but always with the idea of playing an intellectual game; you do not really mean it.

Fifty years later, Christopher Columbus landed in the Canaries. And as the implications of that voyage unfolded themselves, man could no longer wrap himself round in his comfortable European civilization; he found himself sharing an untidy sort of world with a lot of savages—they were all savages to him, Mexicans and Peruvians as much as the rest—whose theology was all wrong, and who could hardly be called to account for it, since the Christian message had never reached them. What had they been doing all the time? Had they discovered the five proofs for themselves? Or, if there was no mute inglorious Aristotle to do that for them, how could they be expected to hold right notions about God? And how was it, almost odder still, that they held any notions at all about God, even wrong ones?

And then, fifty years after that, like a kitten catching sight of its own tail, the philosopher Descartes managed to catch sight of himself thinking, and said to himself, "How do I know that I exist? Only because I think." Everything else became known to him by means of ideas in his own mind; how could he be certain that his ideas corresponded to reality? And so on; he became the father of modern idealism. To him, the idea of God was an idea self-luminous and therefore true; you did not have to prove the existence of God from the existence of the world around you; rather, you had to prove the existence of the world around you from the existence of God. If it were not for the veracity of God, you would have no certainty about anything at all. A well-meaning man and an admirable Catholic; but his system gave birth, in due time, to the sensationalism of Locke and the scepticism of Hume; man began to doubt the value of his own mind as a thinking instrument; and how was he to be sure of the five proofs if he were not certain of his own mental processes?

No thinker ever thinks in complete isolation from the men of his time, even when his thoughts are as lonely as the thoughts of Descartes. He was, in some sense, the child of his age. What had been happening was that the world, miraculously enlarged by Columbus, turned upside down by Copernicus, and suddenly enriched with the rediscovered treasures of classical antiquity, had gone Humanist. Humanism means several things, all of them important; but what is important for our present purpose is that to the Humanist the proper study of mankind is man; what is going on outside you is less interesting than what is going on inside you. Art runs to portrait-painting everywhere, poetry to drama; man occupies the centre of the canvas. And if you were to infer the existence of a Being even greater than man, then it was not to be expected that you should infer it from the nature of the world around you. You would infer it from your own nature, the nature of a thinking being.

Meanwhile, oddly sandwiched between Columbus and Descartes, comes the figure of a third world-disturber, Martin Luther. Reformed Christianity had no quarrel, on the face of it, with natural theology or with the five proofs. But in practice it had no use for either. Man was hopelessly corrupted by the Fall; what was the use to him of having any knowledge about God? No use in knowing God, if you are incapable of pleasing him. And man's only part, the only part which grace allowed him to play, in securing his own salva-

tion was an act of blind faith. Faith was a hand stretched out
to receive the gift of God's mercy; it had no connexion with
the exercise of human reason, depended on no process of
argumentation. So the existence of God was taken to be
something axiomatically true—after all, was it not there, in
the Bible? Only those who were professionally interested in
philosophy worried about the thing any longer.

Nothing marks so clearly the divorce between theology
and philosophy, in the reformed countries especially, as the
rise of Deism. Deism is the philosophical religion of the
seventeenth and eighteenth centuries, a creed which would
admit the existence of a personal Creator, because it can be
proved, but discredits all miracle, all active interference on
the part of Providence, and leaves no room for Christ as a
Divine Figure. Against that you get the protest of Pascal in
France, of Spener and Zinzendorf in Germany, of the
Wesleys in England. The appeal of religion, such men held,
in reaction to the Deists, must be to the heart, not to the
head. Pascal, though he admits the validity of the five proofs,
will not base his apologetic on them or on any other philosophical principle; to convince yourself of the existence of
God without convincing yourself at the same time that you
are a miserable, fallen sinner, is only to add to your unhappi-
ness, and probably to your damnation.

And it was not long before this divorce between theology
and philosophy was followed by a divorce between philosophy and science. An eighteenth-century man of science, like
Newton, was still called a philosopher. The word "scientist"
was only invented in 1840. But it was invented to describe
what had long existed, a class of people who were content to
read the book of nature in the light of experiment, without
bothering about first principles. Philosophy, you see, had
begun the quarrel by doubting the validity of sense experience. But it was a collusive divorce. Men of science, as we
know, are still fond of playing about with philosophy; but
always they are at issue with the philosophers.

So there is our Dominican's pleasant ladder, that once led up straight from creatures to God, broken into three, with cruel gaps between. During the last hundred and fifty years, those philosophers who have argued for the existence of God have usually argued, like Kant, from the nature of the human conscience, or like Hegel, from the nature of human knowledge, not from our experience of the world outside. And theology, among non-Catholics, has become suspicious even of these methods of approach; Kant's moral Arbiter or Hegel's Absolute strikes the religious mind as a chilly abstraction, not easily identified with the personal God we Christians worship. So the modern theologians prefer to tell us that the existence of God is guaranteed to us by experience, whatever exactly that means; or perhaps that the very faculty we have for trembling at the thought of the supernatural world is proof that the supernatural world exists. Anyhow, theology will have her own proofs, even if they do not appear very cogent to the outside world; she will no longer be content to borrow the cast-off clothes of her ugly sister.

Meanwhile, what has the Catholic Church been doing about it all? We do not live in a bay sheltered from every wind that blows; the currents of contemporary thought do create their backwash among ourselves, cherish as we may our own certitudes. There was a tendency, early in the last century, among certain Catholic thinkers to by-pass the old methods of argument. The Fideists maintained that every man, if he will but live up to his opportunities, is provided with a special illumination of faith which tells him that God exists; it is a kind of sixth sense, and there is no argument needed in the matter. Whereas the Traditionalists pointed out that as a matter of common experience the reason why you or I or nearly anybody we meet started believing in God was because we were told about God when we were quite small. After all, presumably Adam told Seth about God, and Seth told Enos, and so on all down the line until finally the revelation made to Adam has reached, by unbroken succession, you and me. Neither of these views has, in its positive side, been condemned. But the Vatican Council in 1870 did fulminate against the negative implication which they were perhaps meant to convey. It reasserted the principle laid down both in the Book of Wisdom and in St Paul's epistle to the Romans that the existence of God can be inferred from consideration of the works which he has made; and to that, as Catholics, we are committed.

This is not, I think, to say that every mind must necessarily recognize the cogency of the five proofs, once they are presented to it. An argument may be in fact valid, without producing more than a languid assent in a mind unaccustomed to breathing the air of metaphysics. It is not, I think, to say that a child abandoned on a desert island and entirely self-taught would necessarily arrive at the truth about God's existence, though I think you have to admit that a society of people, however simple and savage their culture, ought to be able to arrive at it, although no doubt in crude and naïf terms. Certainly it is not to say that all other proofs—the proof from conscience, for example—are invalid, or that a man may not, for his own private purposes, be content with a traditional conviction that God exists, which he never examines further. All it tells us is that if the five proofs do not carry conviction to us, we are not to conclude that they are an exploded mine of medieval thought; we are simply to admit that, probably through stupidity, we don't grasp them.

That is the theory of the situation; what is, in practice, the importance of the five proofs? Well, let us take the thing at its worst; let us suppose that the scholastic approach to the riddle of theology is as remote from real life as its most determined critics would ask us to believe that it is. Let us agree with them, for the sake of argument, in the first place that nobody is, nowadays at any rate, convinced by the five proofs in the sense of altering his religious outlook as the result of coming across them; let us agree, in the second place, that you and I, who have been called to serve God in the Catholic Church,

do better to approach God in a simple spirit of faith than to
remind ourselves by argument that he exists, every time we
put ourselves in his presence and dispose ourselves for prayer.
It is still, I think, important for us to realize that his existence
can be proved, and to clarify our ideas, sometimes, about the
intellectual adventure which that proof involves.

I don't doubt you will have the experience before long, if
you haven't had the experience already, of being present at
some discussion among your non-Catholic friends in which
the fundamental truths of religion will be involved. You will
find, I think, that people who profess themselves to be quite
without belief in God will make allowances for you, as being
a Catholic, in a rather curious way. They will take it for
granted that you have such a belief, and that you cannot be
argued out of it; you are told to believe such and such things,
and of course, you always do what you are told. Nor—this is
the curious thing—do they despise you, as they ought to
despise you, for making such a blasphemous abuse of Almighty God's gift of reason. They have a sort of superstitious
feeling that to be a Catholic is somehow different, makes you
a different sort of person, not just ordinary flesh and blood. I
know what I am talking about, because I can remember
having that feeling about my Catholic friends when I was a
Protestant, although I was a very High Church Protestant,
and I ought to have understood them better. There is a
tendency, somehow, to treat a Catholic as a different kind of
animal; and in a vague way feel as if it were all right for *him*
to believe these things. As if it could ever be right to believe
what is untrue, or as if it were possible for a thing to be true
for one person and not for another!

The danger, as I see it, is that if we are not careful we shall
drift into accepting that estimate of ourselves. That we, on
our side, shall come to think of the unbeliever as a person
who unbelieves because he can't help it—he is made that
way. Now, if you have a reasoned belief in the existence of
God, I don't say that you will be able to bring home convic-

tion to the doubter. But it will protect you, in your own mind, from the danger of thinking that he, being the kind of person he is, has a right to doubt. Nobody has a right to doubt what is true. You will be able to say to yourself, "He and I are not different species of animal; we both live by the same laws of thought, as surely as we breathe the same air. And those laws of thought involve the existence of God; and if this man could get rid of his silly inhibitions he would see that they do." You will be saved from the dangerous error of thinking that religious differences are a matter of taste, instead of a matter of truth.

And in our own lives—well, I suppose it's true that we shan't find ourselves wanting to fall back on the five proofs so long as we are living the life of ordinary Christians. The thought of God is so intertwined with our whole interpretation of the universe, the whole habit of our minds, that we don't have to do more than make an act of faith in God from time to time, and that out of piety rather than from any feeling that we need it. Yes, but there may come a time when, perhaps under the stress of sudden shock, or great disappointment, or unforeseen conflict between your will and God's law, you will be tempted to abandon God, and to take refuge in creatures. Then, if you have borne the yoke of natural theology in your youth, you will see that that is impossible. We cannot think God out of existence simply by wishing him away; he is there. Look down what avenue you will between the tree trunks, you will see his face at the end of it; his creatures report faithfully that he is there. As you look back, over your life, you will be struck by some odd chain of cause and effect in it, and your mind will be carried beyond that to the first Cause, which is God. You will think of the changes which have passed over you, in body and mind, as the years have passed, with nothing but the frail bridge of memory to connect what you are with what you were, and you will see, as the Agent in those changes, the prime Mover, who is God. You will remember the approach of death, and as you reflect on the caducity of your own brief existence you will contrast it with the timeless energy of that necessary Being, who is God. You will feel the pull of some human love, some human admiration, and you will know that the human excellence which evokes it does but point beyond itself to that Supreme Excellence, which is God. You will find yourself a rebel against the order of things, and as you become conscious of the fact, you will realize that there could be no order in things if it were not the expression of a mind, that Mind which is God's. Notice-boards will surround you everywhere to tell you that there is no way out this way. Whether you want him or not, God is there.

3

The Average Man's Doubts about God

I don't feel any hesitation about discussing the average man's doubts about God; doubts which I can view with sympathy and—I hope you won't misunderstand me when I say this—which I share. Let me linger on that point for a moment. Strictly speaking, theologically speaking, a Christian has no doubts. And when we condescend to discuss the question whether Almighty God exists, the books tell us that we are only putting before ourselves a "methodical" doubt; we use the words "supposing God didn't exist", just as we might use the words, "supposing Japhet had fallen out of the Ark"; we are simply, for the sake of argument, imagining an impossibility. That's all right, on paper. On paper, our motives for believing what we do believe are such as to exclude all reasonable doubt. But the thing isn't really quite as simple as that, is it?

Doubt is something that gets in under the skin. I remember once when I was being treated by a doctor who went in very much for injections, he said a rather startling thing by way of explaining what injections were and did. He said, "I've got pneumonia, myself", and then proceeded to explain that he had got all the right germs for pneumonia wandering about in his system, but they were being held in check, neutralized, by the injections he had given himself. Well, if a doctor can talk like that, you mustn't be shocked by a priest saying he can "share" the doubts which stupid people have about the existence of God. You and I have got all the apparatus in us for doubting every article of the Christian creed; faith is not a knife which cuts them out; it is an injection which neutralizes them. Many of us have bad times, perhaps when we wake up at four in the morning and can't go to sleep again, when the whole of religion *seems* absolutely unreal to us. And at such times we don't merely see the point of the atheist's line of argument, we feel the attraction of it. And at such moments it bothers stupid people like you and me—I mean, stupid people like some of you and me— that we seem to have lost the hang of that apologetic we learned at school and thought we had got word-perfect. Well, so as to be ready for the next time that happens, let's just go over the old ground, and see what it really was we were supposed to learn at school, and what we really assimilated, and whether that was the part most worth assimilating. What a tricky thing memory is! When you are at school, you always seem to forget the thing you were taught yesterday. By the time you are fifty, you find it impossible to remember anything except what you were taught at school.

I think most of us would have to admit that when we did apologetics for the first time, and were told about the five classical proofs of God's existence, there were two which really seized upon our imaginations, the first two; our only doubt about them was whether they were two or only one. I suppose, after all, the argument from Motion appealed to us, unconsciously, just because it so vividly recalled a situation which was a matter of almost daily experience to us in those days. I mean the situation in which you push somebody else because somebody else pushes you. You were standing on the touch-line at some terribly exciting point of the match, and in order to see what was happening a bit further along it was necessary to support yourself by the shoulders of the boy immediately in front of you. That was all right as far as it went; but then some silly fool behind began to support himself by *your* shoulders; and that disturbed the equilibrium of the thing, and you all three fell forward and got in the way just as the ball was coming along, and angry monitors clustered round and asked what on earth you thought you were doing. So it didn't need much imagination, when you got into the apologetics class, to picture the whole of existence as a series of things each of which was pushing the thing in front because it was being pushed by the thing behind. Well, obviously that kind of thing couldn't go on for ever; if nothing ever moved anything except because something else moved it, sooner or later you got back to a primal source of motion, and that source of motion had to be looked for beyond the range of ordinary terrestrial existence, and so you had to believe in the existence of a God.

And there was another situation with which you were equally familiar, being blamed for something, and managing to put the blame on somebody else. You couldn't find your book, just as you were going into class, so you borrowed one from your next-door neighbour, and when he got into trouble for not having a book, he told the master that was because you had borrowed his book, and you told the master that was because somebody else had borrowed yours, and so on and so on. But it couldn't be and so on and so on *ad infinitum*; every boy had a book, or was supposed to have a book, and therefore the transaction couldn't, in the last resort, be explained by an infinite series of borrowing; sooner or later you must get down to the boy who had left his book in the swimming-bath. That sort of experience enabled you to sympathize with the argument from causation. Everything in existence behaved as it did because it was influenced by the way in which something else behaved; and that something else behaved as it did because it was influenced by the way in which something else behaved, and so on and so on; but once more it couldn't be and so on and so on *ad infinitum*. Sooner or later you must arrive at a first Cause, outside our series of terrestrial causes, which was responsible for the behaviour of all the others. And you couldn't feel happy until you had found the ultimate source of all causation in God.

I don't say that you had properly appreciated all the nuances of the doctrine. You probably, for example, pictured the whole thing to yourself as happening in time; and just because your imagination was too idle to go back and back and back in the direction of an infinite past, you decided to call a halt somewhere and say, "No, dash it all, the thing must have started some time!" But in theory, of course, there is no reason why you shouldn't have an infinite series of events each of which is the cause of the next. The real philosophical objection is that even if you had an infinite series of causes each dependent on the last, you wouldn't have arrived at an explanation. It would be like a chain with an infinite series of rings, which still couldn't hang unless, somewhere, there is a peg. But all that didn't worry you; you took the two first arguments in your stride. And after that, you felt inclined to sit back and take a rest. That third proof, for example; necessary being and contingent being— that sounded too much like work. And the argument from degrees of excellence just didn't seem to add up; if you could argue from the fact that one thing is better than another to the existence of something supremely good, why shouldn't you argue from the fact that one thing is hotter than another to the existence of something supremely hot? As to the argument from order, that was all right, of course, but it was rather a kid's argument; it reminded you of nursery days when you were told that God fed the poor little dicky-birds, without personally feeling very much interested whether the poor little dicky-birds were fed or not. On the whole, it was the first two proofs you liked best, and remembered longest.

That is all the more unfortunate, because these two proofs, lucid as is the logic of them, are a favourite target for criticism; and it is the kind of criticism which you are almost certain to come across among your friends up here, if you develop the habit of talking what we used to call Greats-shop to them. There is a difficult objection which can be urged in each case. I don't say it's an insuperable objection; there are lots of people very much cleverer than myself who would say it's mere child's play to get rid of it. All I say is that it is fairly easy to understand the objection, and not nearly so easy to see the force of the come-back. And this morning, speaking as a stupid person to those of you who labour under the same shortcomings as myself, I'm bound to take that into account. Because an objection to which we can't understand the answer is, for us, just as bad as an objection to which there is no answer at all. On those uncomfortable occasions when we wake up at four in the morning and can't get to sleep again, an unsolved objection is as bad as an insoluble one.

What the objector tells us is this. We have offered him a syllogism, something of this kind: Every effect has a cause; total nature is an effect; therefore total nature has a cause. But, they say, our syllogism has a concealed flaw. It really ought to run: Every effect has a natural, instrumental cause; total nature is an effect; therefore total nature has a supernatural, efficient cause. In other words, we have side-stepped from physics into metaphysics. And even if scientists were given to talking about causes and effects (which as a matter of fact, says the objector, they aren't nowadays), you would have no right to assume that a principle which holds good inside nature holds good equally outside nature. Moreover, in calling total nature an effect, you have begged the question. Moreover, you yourselves admit that God does not belong to any category. Yet in your syllogism you have put him into a category; you have made him one of the causes.

I don't say I've stated the objection right, but it's that sort of thing. I don't, as I say, suggest that there isn't a come-back, I only say that it bothers me when the whole argument resolves itself into a discussion about whether metaphysics exist at all, and people start talking about the blind man in the dark room looking for the black cat that isn't there. That is the point in the discussion at which I slide out of the room and say I've got to put out the vestments for tomorrow. What do I fall back on instead? Well, of course there is always the fifth proof, or fourth proof if you number them the other way, the proof from Order. No order which isn't the expression of a mind, but there *is* order in the universe, therefore the universe must be the expression of a mind. But there's a fresh crab about that proof, if I'm not mistaken. I mean, it's all right to claim that the adaptation of means to ends which we find in the natural creation can't be the result of mere chance; it argues the existence of an organizing Mind. But you can't prove that that Mind *is* the Supreme Being. It has been held, before now, that the Universe was created not by the Supreme Being, but by a very inferior kind of angelic intelligence. What *do* I fall back on, then? I mean, when I'm lying awake at four o'clock in the morning? I haven't got it all clear in my own mind, but I want to try and tell you.

I suggest that we should put on one side the question, whether the existence of God can be proved, by direct logical inference, from our knowledge of the world about us. That we should ask ourselves instead, whether the existence of God is not an apprehension which comes to us in and through our knowledge of the world about us, and (still more) in and through the knowledge we have of ourselves. No, I am not going to say we have an immediate intuition of God's existence; that is doubtful philosophy, and also doubtful theology. I am suggesting that the knowledge of God is something which emerges from our knowledge of life, although for the life of us we can't quite see how it got there. Does that sound wholly paradoxical? Tell me, then, how do we get our notion of solid objects, when we can only see in two dimensions? How do we get our notion of reality, when our experience consists of nothing but a series of sense-impressions? How do we get our notion of right and wrong, when our natural faculties of appreciation only tell us that some things are fun and some aren't? How is it that we always find ourselves putting a construction on our experience which isn't exactly part of that experience, yet obviously isn't something we just *put* there? Abt Vogler was wrong if he thought music was quite different from everything else:

> I know not if, save in this, such gift is allowed to man,
>   That out of three sounds he frame, not a fourth sound,
>   but a star.

On the contrary, we are always doing it.

I suggest, then, that in order to look at the world sanely we have to think of the world, not as something which exists in its own right, but as deriving its existence from Something outside of and higher than itself; as essentially dependent, derivative, factitious. And, as a man confronted by some astonishing sight will rub his eyes to make sure that he is awake, not dreaming, so we, faced with this necessity of reading into the world about us a meaning which is not apparently there, put our state of mind not to one test, but to a series of tests. And those tests are the five proofs which we get in our manuals of scholastic philosophy.

The important one is the third—the one we couldn't be bothered about at school, because it looked too high-brow. Can I really suppose that I myself, or the world about me, exists *necessarily*, that the non-existence of it is something *inconceivable*? Or, again, can I think of the changes that take place in it, changes of position, changes of state, as producing themselves? Can I really think of all the events in it as determined by the spin of a coin, although in fact there is no coin, and nobody there to spin it? Can I really think of the beauty, the goodness I see about me as merely an affection of my own tastes, and not as the reflection of a Beauty, a Goodness, which lies beyond themselves? Can I really think of all the order I trace in it as something which my mind puts into it, and not rather as something which my mind finds in it? It's not like a photographer taking five different snaps, to make sure of one being right even if the other four get fogged. It's like an artist squinting through his fist from five different points of view to make sure that the picture he has built up of his sitter is the right one.

I think you can say that holds good, too, of the other proofs which don't occur on St Thomas's list. The argument from conscience, for example, is really an application of the same principle; how to suppose that the august deliveries of morality really take their origin in perishable wills like ours? Or the argument that you can't really explain the relation between the thinking mind and the object thought about, except in terms of a higher reality which transcends both. Some of these arguments, not from our experience of the outside world, but from the consciousness of our own thought-processes, go very near to being satisfactory even when you take them by themselves. But I think for us stupid people it's cosier—let's put it like that—to think of all these proofs, not as being necessarily cogent in themselves, but as being fresh observations to assure us that the God-dependent construction we put on the universe is the right one.

Meanwhile, I think this way of looking at things makes it easier for us to dispose of certain incidental difficulties which are apt to puzzle us in those early-morning meditations. The old difficulty, for instance: How is it that so many clever people don't believe in God, if his existence can be so convincingly demonstrated? You see, by our way of it, the first step in the whole process is to have a sane view of life. And these clever people aren't always in that position. They may be logical enough, learned enough, sensitive enough to artistic impressions, but—think of a few atheists, not casual atheists, I mean, but crass atheists, and ask yourself whether you really regard them as a very *sane* set of people? That other difficulty, too, about how the people who simply can't cope with logic at all, people even stupider than you and me, can be expected to believe in God. The answer is that all these logical arguments aren't really the way in which we find out God, but merely tests by which we assure ourselves, at need, that our observations were correct. Perhaps the very very stupid people don't need them.

And at the same time I think it helps to rid us of that uneasy suspicion that the God of religion is one thing and the God of philosophy another; or, to put it more accurately, perhaps, that the God of religion is a Person and the God of philosophy is a Thing. There is something curiously desic-cated and unsatisfactory, isn't there, about those titles by which Almighty God is referred to in the manuals of apologetics? You've only to substitute them for the name of God in phrases taken from ordinary life, to assure you of that. "For the sake of the First Cause, do turn that gramaphone off . . . Well, good-bye, old man, the Prime Mover bless you . . . I'm not a narrow-minded man, the Supreme Intelligence knows"— that kind of thing. But if all that is only subsidiary; if the doctrine of Creation is a guess man's mind was made to leap at, a spark that flies out unbidden from the anvil of experi-ence; then you get a different angle on the whole process. Then there is no time-lag between your discovery that God exists, and the reflection that you ought to do something about it. You apprehend, with one grasp of the mind, earth's inadequacy and God's all-sufficiency; you see yourself, earth-born, in the true perspective, and read, written in between the lines of all our human record, the attestation of a God whom to acknowledge is to adore.

4

Our Knowledge of God by Analogy

I think the ordinary reaction of a mind which has been introduced, for the first time, to the scholastic proofs of God's existence, the argument from the first Cause and the argument from the Prime Mover and so on, is to say, "Thank you very much; and now, tell me, is God a Person, or a Thing?" After all, a Cause is only a thing, and an abstract thing at that; and although in Latin the word "motor" suggests a personal agent, we who talk English associate the word "motor" with a thing. Meanwhile (you say), before I start saying prayers to him I want to be sure that God is a Person; is he? Well, of course that is badly put. God can't very well be a Person, or how could he be Three? Let us restate the question by asking, Is the God of philosophy a personal God? Is there room for personality in any metaphysical notion of the Divine Nature?

The first answer to that, our immediate reaction, is Yes. Because after all the stream doesn't rise higher than its source, and God, however we conceive him, must be higher in the scale of being than anything he has created. And among his creatures, persons are higher in the scale of being than things. As I seem to remember putting it elsewhere, you can look up into the sky and say, "That's the planet Venus", but the planet Venus can't look down and say, "That's Mary Jane." Only the existence of persons gives the world of things its significance; without persons, it would be quite uninteresting, because there would be nobody to take an interest in it. Of course, you can try to gain time by using the word "matter" instead of the word "things", and the word "spirit" instead of the word "persons". God may be a Spirit, you object, without being a Person. But, you see, we've got to argue from the data of our experience, and in our experience a spirit and a person are inseparable; they are two ways of saying the same thing. When we talk about the spirit of democracy, or say that there's a good spirit among the University Ping-Pong team, we are only using a metaphor, we are only talking about something abstract. To suppose that God was a Spirit in that abstract sense wouldn't meet our difficulty; abstractions don't create. If we call him a Spirit in the concrete sense we are, by that very fact, crediting him with personality.

That is the first way in which, by the light of the natural reason, we can know something about God, over and above the bare fact of his existence. It is called the way of causation, or sometimes the way of affirmation. If a creature is such and such, its Creator must be such and such, or he couldn't have created it. That doesn't apply, of course, to all the limited existences we see around us; it would be absurd to say that God must be a tree, or he couldn't have made trees, that God must be a snake, or he couldn't have made snakes. No, but the excellent qualities we find in our experience, which look as if they could be multiplied to the *nth* without ceasing to be themselves, those, surely, must belong to God *a fortiori*, since they belong to us. Surely he must be wise, surely he must be good. As the Psalm says, "Is he deaf, the God who implanted hearing in us; is he blind, the God who gave us eyes to see?" That, surely, is common sense.

That's the way of affirmation; and almost the moment we set our feet on it, a scruple assails us, and we want to take it all back. Supposing that King David, instead of writing the verse I quoted just now, had written like this: "Has he no ear-drums, the God who implanted hearing in us? Has he no retina, the God who gives us eyes to see?"—it wouldn't sound so well, would it? In fact, it would be nonsense. We

can't think of Almighty God as really having physical organs
like ourselves, however much the Bible may talk as if he had.
And something of the same sort applies, even when we as-
cribe abstract perfections to him. Has he really got "personality"? Think what that ordinarily means to us; a man's
personality is built up out of a thousand tricks of heredity
and human background; it marks him off from his fellows—
"Personally," you say, "I don't care for the wireless", as if to
mark yourself off from a whole lot of other people who do.
We can think of God as having personality; can we think of
him as having *a* personality? And so it is with all the attributes
we assign to him; we can't really think of Almighty God as
falling into the same category as his creatures, wise as
Aristotle was wise, only rather more so, good as St Francis
was good, only rather more so. Nothing can be predicated in
the same sense of an infinite Creator and his finite creatures.
And so we reach the second way by which we attain knowledge of God, the way of negation. God is not such and such;
not what we mean by wise, not what we mean by good.

And that brings us on to the third way, the way of eminence. We have committed ourselves to two statements:
"God has got personality", "God hasn't got personality". And
the only way we can make sense of that contradiction is to
say, "God has got super-personality". I wish we hadn't vul-
garized that prefix "super" in our disgusting modern way of
talking. Somebody will offer you a lump of super-toffee; all
that means is that it is toffee only rather more so, a bit sweeter
and a bit tastier than other toffees on the market. But, as we
were remarking just now, that turn of speech "only rather
more so" is hopelessly out of place when you are talking
about God and his creatures. The theologians tell us that God
is eminently good, is eminently wise; we say, perhaps, that
the air of Switzerland is eminently suited to those who are
suffering from pulmonary complaints; are we using the same
language? Certainly not; we mean that the air of Switzerland
is healthy as compared with others; the theologian doesn't

mean that God is good or wise as compared with his creatures, he means that God is good or wise in a quite different
sense from his creatures, in a way which his creatures cannot
even imagine.

That's all right, then, for our own immediate purposes.
When we say that God is, for instance, beautiful, we are
saying three things. He is beautiful, or he could not have
created a world of beauty; he is not beautiful, for we think of
beauty in terms of form and colour and line, which do not
apply in this case; he is more than beautiful, there is in him a
beauty which to us is simply unimaginable. And that would
be enough, if we were merely speaking within four walls; we
talk the language of scholastic philosophy, and if it was good
enough for St Thomas it is good enough for us. But when
you start talking like that to your tutor, you'll find it doesn't
go down very well.

You see, we call this process the knowledge of God through
analogy. And your tutor probably doesn't distinguish in his
mind between analogy and metaphor. We do use metaphor,
of course, and use it quite legitimately, when we are talking
about religion. Abbot Hunter-Blair used to have a description of a Scottish minister who was preaching about "The
Lord is my shepherd." He started off, "You see, my dear
friends, I'm your shepherd", and then he pointed at the clerk,
who was sitting just below the pulpit; "I'm your shepherd",
he said, "and yon's ma wee doggie." And the clerk screwed his
neck round to look up at the pulpit, and said, "I'm thinking
I'm no your wee doggie." To which the minister was forced
to reply, "Hoot, mon, I was only speaking metaphorical." So
he was, and so we often do when we talk about Almighty
God; the Old Testament is full of it. Quite often you hear of
Almighty God being pleased with the smell of a burnt
sacrifice; and all *that* means is that he was as much pleased by
the faith and dutifulness of the people who offered the
sacrifice, as a man would be pleased by the smell of dinner
cooking—not that I'm very fond of the smell of overdone

meat myself, but I suppose that is a matter of taste. And it's the same, of course, when the Bible talks about God being angry; it means that his eternal justice demanded punishment, in the measure in which the injured feelings of an angry man would demand punishment. I don't suppose you or I ever say a prayer without using metaphor.

Now, if so much of what we say about God is metaphorical, mightn't it be suggested that all we say about God is metaphorical? If, when we talk about his being angry, we only mean that he behaves as an angry man would, what about calling him merciful? Do we perhaps only mean that he behaves as a merciful man would? When we call him wise or good, do we mean that he really possesses those qualities, or do we mean that for some reason, unknown to us, he behaves towards us as a wise or good man would behave? And if that is all we mean, do we really know anything about his nature at all? That is where we have to insist on the difference between metaphor and analogy. It is a metaphor if you describe Oxford as a hive of industry, or some of its inhabitants as drones. You don't mean to imply that undergraduates are driven to lectures by an uncontrollable impulse, such as that which drives the bees out to make honey; you don't cast any stigma on the drones, which hang about doing nothing because it is their nature to; it is only a metaphor. But if you describe the Empress Catherine as the Semiramis of the North, or Tenby as the Mentone of South Wales, it is no longer a metaphor but an analogy. You mean that the same quality was evinced by two different women in vastly different ages and circumstances; you mean that the same balmy atmosphere is to be met with in two quite different parts of Europe.

The moment we have said that, the moment we have said good-bye to metaphor, we are greeted with a great shout of "Anthropomorphism!" To suggest that any quality which resides in us does really reside also in Almighty God, is simply to put yourself out of court with some of these people; you

are simply fashioning God in your own image, representing
him as nothing more than a very good man up in the sky.
You might as well use the language of the fish in Rupert
Brooke's poem:

> Mud unto mud! Death eddies near;
> Not here the appointed end, not here!
> But somewhere, beyond space and time,
> Is wetter water, slimier slime!
> And there, they trust, there swimmeth One
> Who swam ere rivers were begun,
> Immense, of fishy form and mind,
> Squamous, omnipotent, and kind;
> And under that almighty Fin
> The littlest fish may enter in.[1]

And, very patiently, we have to go on, saying, "No, that isn't
what we mean at all. It isn't a question of wetter water and
slimier slime; of things being the same in God, only more so.
Of course we don't imagine that the Divine attributes are
something which we can conceive for ourselves by merely
doing a multiplication sum. No, goodness and wisdom are
present in the Divine Nature after an entirely different manner, one which we can't represent to ourselves by any gym-
nastics of human thought—how should we? We are men, not
God, not angels even. All we know is that they must be
there."

And then, of course, we are attacked from the other angle.
"Very well, then," they say, "what it comes to is that you are
agnostics after all, just as we are. True, by certain metaphysical processes you have inferred the existence of Something
which you call God, but we prefer to call X, because after all
it's an unknown quantity. When we ask you what X is like

---

[1] Reprinted by permission of Dodd, Mean & Company from *Collected Poems
of Rupert Brooke*. Copyright 1915 by Dodd, Mead & Company, Inc.

you start off by giving us a long list of things which he isn't; he is immortal, invisible, incomprehensible, immutable, without passions, unaffected by space or time; presumably you are not going to say, at the end of this long litany of negations, that you have, so far, any knowledge about God? And then, when we ask for something more positive, you tell us that he is good and wise, and so on, but then you tell us in the next breath that you've no idea what you mean when you talk in that way. What it comes to is that you are confessing complete ignorance; you are merely attaching a string of *names* to X, and you have no more information at the end of it than a belligerent power has when its spies report that the enemy's next move is called Operation Mulberry. Go on praying to X if you like, but let us have no more of your theologies. If you want to speculate you had much better speculate about the square root of minus one."

And at this point they don't fail to throw the mystics up at us. The mystics, even some of the quite orthodox ones, rather sell the pass when it comes to this question of how we know anything about God, by saying that we don't—or something precious like it. When we address our prayers to Almighty God, if we will adopt their recipe, we must dismiss from our minds all theological considerations; we mustn't think of him under any title, or in terms of any attribute, we mustn't represent him by any symbol. We cling to the naked thought of God, present here and now to something in us that is beyond the intellect, beyond even the will, the peak or base (you may call it which you will) of the human spirit. "If by chance thou e'er shalt doubt where to turn in search of me, seek not all the world about, only this can find me out—thou must find myself in thee." That is the mystical approach, and even St Thomas, after all, had an ecstasy shortly before his death which made him tell Brother Reginald that all the theology he had written seemed worthless by comparison. If St Thomas can be cited as a death-bed convert from intellectualism, why should

Christian people go on reading the *Summa*, go on grinding
out its conclusions, as if from a barrel-organ, in the lecture-
rooms of every seminary in the world?

I haven't left myself much time to answer myself, but I
must just indicate the flaws in that argument. First of all, is it
certain that we get no positive knowledge out of saying,
"God isn't this . . . God isn't that . . . God isn't that"? Oh, I
know it's bad form in logic, or used to be, to use negative
terms in a definition. All the same, you will find it pretty
hard to define a point or a line without using negative terms
over it. And in this case, you see, the things we are denying
about God are really negative things; they are defects in our
nature which limit us and make us something less than we
might be. When the hymn for None tells us that God is
motionless, that description would also apply, in popular language at any rate, to a piece of rock. But the rock is motionless because it can't move; God is motionless because he has
no need to move; he can be everywhere without moving; in
him, it is not the absence of a perfection, but the absence of a
defect. And is the absence of a defect really something negative? Oh, to be sure, we have to think of it as something
negative, because our own minds are limited. But our want
of intelligence is due not to darkness, but to excess of light.
What we have said is something frighteningly positive.

And when it comes to those other perfections of the Divine Being, which we describe in positive terms, is it really
true that our analogies make us none the wiser? Remember
the story of the blind man, blind from his birth, when they
tried to explain to him about colour. They tried with scarlet
first of all, and what they said I don't know, but at the end of
it he remarked, "Oh, I think I've got it; it must be rather like
the sound of a trumpet". Now, that wasn't a metaphor; you
have to know both of the terms you're dealing with before
you can construct a metaphor. No, it was an analogy, and
obviously it was true as far as it went; the effect of scarlet on
the eye is rather like the effect of a trumpet-blast on the ear.

He had got hold of something, and we have got hold of something when we say God is good or God is wise; our statement is true as far as it goes, although our limited conceptions make it impossible for us to realize how staggeringly true it is.

And the mystics, God bless them, the mystics know that just as well as you or I do. If they don't think about the wisdom or the goodness of God in their prayer, it's because they don't think about anything in their prayer; if you are a mystic, to start thinking is to stop praying. But their whole approach to God, that of the Christian mystics anyhow, is conditioned through and through by this dim apperception we all have of what God is like. Just in the same way, they don't think about their own sins, while they are praying, although they are much more conscious of sin than you and I are. God's goodness, their sinfulness, are taken as real; they are present to the mind in the same sort of way in which the fact that you have just won a scholarship is present to the mind when you are listening to a concert. In the very highest stages, no doubt, a great saint like St Thomas may be privileged by the lifting of a curtain which gives him a more direct view of the other world. But it would be ridiculous to suppose that St Thomas, when he came round from his ecstasy, had ceased to believe in the *Summa*. No, he had only realized more vividly than ever, what he was never tired of telling us in the *Summa*, that the knowledge of God which we get by analogy is hopelessly inadequate.

Our intellects stammer and boggle when they try to reach the truth about Divine things, not because the other world is a reflection of ours, but because ours is a reflection, and how pale a reflection, of the other. That was what our Lord wanted us to see when he turned our metaphors, even, inside out for us, as you may read in St John. The water in Jacob's well isn't real water; the real water is the living fountain of grace which he will unseal for the woman of Samaria, if she will only stop to listen. The vine that grows on yonder wall is not a real vine; the only real Vine is his own mystical body. The things we see and touch are only the shadows cast by eternal truth. What marvel if we, to whom shadow is substance, cannot raise our minds to contemplate the substance by which that shadow is cast?

5

Survival after Death

As Christians, we are bound to believe in a life beyond death, because the Church assures us that there is such a thing. But whether we could form any ideas about that apart from revelation, by the mere use of human reason, is a different question altogether, and you are quite at liberty to hold that one can't.

What should we think about immortality, if we had no Christian revelation to guide us? Well, isn't that the same as asking what people did believe about immortality before they had any Christian revelation to guide them? Unfortunately, it isn't as simple as all that. When you read about a savage king in some primitive country being buried with his favourite wife and his favourite cook and his bow and arrows and his dog, your immediate thought is, "Why, these people must have believed in immortality." But the thing isn't certain; it may have been important to ensure that the favourite wife shouldn't want her husband to predecease her, and (if there was any suspicion of poison) that would go equally for the favourite cook. If a Roman householder walked round his property once a year, spitting black beans over his shoulder and shouting, "Go away, ghosts of my fathers", he may have been convinced of immortality, or he may have been simply taking no risks. Even where you have literary records, it is hard to know whether Homer, for instance, really believed in Hades or whether it was just poetry. You can't construct an accurate picture of ancient beliefs from the records that have come down to us, any more than you could construct an accurate account of modern American beliefs from *The Loved One.*

Still, if you are inclined to attach much importance to a straw vote in matters of this kind, I think, you've got to say that the Ayes have it. The older civilizations, in Egypt and China and so on, either show belief in immortality or else (perhaps more importantly) show traces of an earlier belief in immortality which has degenerated, as time went on, into mere funeral conventions. (Thus, if some antiquarian of the future dug up a copy of *The Loved One*, he might be puzzled to know whether the Americans of the twentieth century believed in immortality, but he would be certain that their ancestors had.) And a belief so widely spread does suggest either a common instinct of mankind or a common tradition of mankind on the subject. But, if it is an instinct, the question immediately arises, "Have I got it?" If I have, my instinct is probably more important to me than other people's. And if I haven't, it will probably make me more impatient than ever of other people's notions on the subject; instincts which other people have and one hasn't got oneself always seem rather fishy. On the other hand, if it's a tradition, we still don't know when it started or where it came from. It would be very nice to believe that Adam told Seth all about it, and Seth told Enos, and so it has come down to you and me. But, if that were so, we should expect the belief in immortality to be specially prominent in the Old Testament, and as a matter of fact the Old Testament rather lets us down. There aren't a great many direct references to personal survival after death, and the most convincing of them come in books which belong to a comparatively late period, at or after the time of the Babylonian captivity. One way or another, I think you have to admit that the straw-vote argument is only a suasion, not a proof exactly, and that it's very much a matter of temperament how powerful a suasion you feel it to be. So let's treat the subject this morning as if we were living on a desert island, and had no information about the future life at all, except what we can derive from the contemplation of our own mental processes.

Well, let's start by putting the case against survival after death. I haven't been at pains, in thinking out this conference, to read up a whole lot of books by atheists. Because the atheist can't prove that death means extinction; you can't prove a negative; you can't sit round in the dark and call up spirits to tell you that they don't exist, can you? Or, to put it in another way, suppose some old lady in North Oxford whose dog has been run over by a 'bus tells you that her dog isn't really dead, it's only passed on to the Happy Hunting-grounds, how are you going to prove to her that she's wrong? No, the argument against immortality isn't a piece of philosophical reasoning worked out by a set of deep thinkers in Moscow. It's a thing that naturally occurs to quite ordinary people like you and me when we wake up at four in the morning after a heavy dinner the night before; we can work it all out for ourselves. And it isn't, as I say, exactly an argument; it's a composite picture which we build up for ourselves out of stray pieces of experience; like what Father D'Arcy calls "indirect reference"—at least, I think that's what he means by indirect reference. Rather as a poem is built up out of a lot of stray thoughts which don't at first sight seem as if they had much to do with one another—at least, not if it's a modern poem they don't.

Waking and sleeping—the subject which chiefly occupies your thoughts at four o'clock in the morning—doesn't even that daily phenomenon suggest that the soul is only a sort of appendage, a sort of excrescence on the body? Somebody comes along with a wet sponge and dabs it down on your face, and all at once your soul comes into action again, having been apparently off-duty for the past eight hours. You can switch it on as you would switch on an electric light, but you have to do it through the body—the body is the dominant partner, not the soul. The body has been lying there, living its own life, the heart beating, the lungs working, the hair growing, quite happy without any conscious soul to look after it; and the conscious soul has been in abeyance, or at best wandering (only for a few moments, they tell us) in an unreal world of dreams. The soul only exists, if we may put it in that way, by courtesy of the body.

And then, how easily the body can influence the soul! I remember once, as an undergraduate, sitting up very late at night talking about the influence of mind over matter; and when we had all got worked up to the verge of Spiritualism, I remember that I mixed myself a very stiff hot whiskey, remarking, "I'm going to try a little of the influence of matter over mind." Most of us are familiar, if only at second hand, with the effects of what my doctor calls concentrated alcohol on the thought-processes; how the shyest person in the room turns into a Mohawk, and the most brilliant conversationalist into a bore. The whole character, the whole personality is changed—how? Why, by dint of pouring some liquid down a hole in the face. And that consideration leads on to drugs, real drugs; how is it that the soul can experience a change from hell to heaven when the body has been pricked with a needle? The soul, surely, if it is so much at the body's mercy, must be held to exist only by courtesy of the body.

And then, there's worse than that—terrible accidents which affect the brain and make the mind wander; perhaps have such a permanent effect that the memory of the past only comes back in a distorted form, and for practical purposes the man who ran into that lorry is a different man ever afterwards. Death itself, I mean the business of dying, reinforces this impression that bodily weakness can impair the very structure of the soul; how frail are the anchors which bind the dying man to his surroundings, to his past! The mental powers seem to be failing progressively, like the water running away out of a bath; and shall we not believe that when the last separation comes, they have failed altogether?

All those experiences help to build up our picture of what death means; and of course there are lots of other puzzling things which enhance the effect. Have congenital idiots really got souls? If the soul is really there all the time, how is it that the mental life of a child develops by such gradual stages? Can all these millions of people in the world, and in the world's past, many of them so pointless, so underdeveloped, really be fit for the experience of eternity?—and so on. But at the back of it all there is one difficulty, presenting itself under a hundred different forms: If there is really a thing called the soul, why are its activities so largely borrowed? Must we not conclude, when all is said and done, that the soul exists by courtesy of the body?

That is our picture. Of course, we haven't been talking philosophical language; one doesn't think in philosophical language at four o'clock in the morning. We have been talking of the soul as if it were identical with consciousness; and though we only know of the soul's existence through our consciousness, you can't just identify the two like that. We can't say there is any reason in the nature of things why the soul should not continue to live for centuries without any awareness whatsoever. But it is consciousness we are interested in; we want to know about conscious survival, not just any sort of survival, after death. What I want to submit is that all these impressions of ours about body and soul, though they are natural enough because the body is so very much present to us, especially at four o'clock in the morning, are in fact exquisitely wrong. The inferences we ought to have been drawing are the exact opposite of the inferences we drew.

In the first place, we tried to make out that the soul couldn't really be important, because it was only a kind of appendage of the body. When we talked like that, we were using the language of teleology, of the end or purpose for which things exist; otherwise the word "important" wouldn't have come into it. Such language is unfashionable nowadays, but still, we have been using it; we have appealed to teleology, to teleology we must go. Our argument was that the body could get on, at a pinch, without the soul, but the soul couldn't get on without the body, and therefore the body must be the more important of the two partners. And evidently it is true that the human body could get on without its intellectual soul. If the whole human race had their intellectual souls removed, and were provided with animal souls in exchange, we shouldn't do too badly in the struggle for existence. Just at first perhaps we shouldn't be handy enough in shinning up trees, but we should soon learn. Whereas, for the purposes of the material world in which we live, the soul would be absolutely lost without the body; it would have no means of expressing itself. Even if you believe in Spiritualism it doesn't work out at much more than going round making noises with the furniture. The body is more useful to the soul than the soul is to the body; so what? Why, obviously the soul, not the body, is the really important thing about us. The switch exists for the sake of the light, not the light for the sake of the switch. The pipe exists for the sake of the smoke, not the smoke for the sake of the pipe. The organ exists for the sake of the music, not the music for the sake of the organ. And by the same reasoning we ought to have concluded that the body exists for the sake of the soul, not the soul for the sake of the body.

And again, we argued that the soul must be something brittle and derivative, if it could be so affected by any abnormal condition of the material brain. That a mere knock on the head should produce unconsciousness, banishing (it seemed) the soul from the body; should produce a loss of memory, total or partial, so that one of the three faculties of the soul remained in abeyance, as it were; should produce derangement of the mind, so that the person concerned was no longer mentally recognizable as the same person—if the soul was so vulnerable by assaults made on the body, why should we not suppose that it suffers when the body suffers death? All that sounds plausible enough, but in fact we were making, once again, the wrong inferences. Supposing that, by some careless movement, you knock over the standard lamp which is the only illumination in your room; it falls with a heavy crash, but you pick it up without taking much notice; it is still daylight. Then, at night, you come back and turn on the switch, and the room remains in darkness. Do you say to yourself, "What! Another of these power cuts!"? Not unless you are a fool. And we were really fools, in exactly the same way, when we tried to draw conclusions about the nature of the soul from the effect which is produced by injuries to the brain. Your lamp won't light because the receiving instrument is wrong, not because there is any shortage of power; the victim of an accident suffers loss of memory or of consciousness, or starts behaving oddly, because the brain, the receiving instrument, is wrong; we have no right to conclude anything about the soul. What has happened is something like what happens when you can hear the person at the other end of the telephone, and he can't hear you; what happens when you put a record on the gramophone forgetting that it has practically run down. There is something wrong with the machine—but only with the machine.

And so it is, surely, with these other mental lapses we were considering. The drunk man behaves oddly, and perhaps a tactful landlady will tell you that he is not quite himself. But she is wrong; he is all too much himself—only it is a different side of himself to what appears when he is sober. Drunkenness doesn't affect the will; all it does is to neutralize the action of those brakes which ordinarily inhibit us. It is still the machine that is at fault. And when the machine fails altogether, when the body first grows motionless, then decays, what is happening to the soul? It is destroyed, you say—but how? Certainly God could annihilate it, as he could annihilate any of his creatures; but in the natural course of things why should it, how could it, be destroyed? All the idea of destruction we have in our minds is, when you come to think of it, of things being dissolved into their component parts; but has the soul got any component parts to be dissolved into? Memory, understanding and will aren't three layers stuck on the top of one another like a Neapolitan ice; our experience is of ourselves remembering, ourselves thinking, ourselves willing, and the self is a pin-point—what is it going to dissolve into? That is how the philosophers, only in more learned language, try to comfort us, when we get that four-o'clock-in-the-morning feeling. And I've never been able to see how you get past it. Oh, I know there are people who will talk about losing your personal identity and getting merged in a world-soul; but that's all just metaphor, and metaphor only derived from our knowledge of material things. When you get down to hard facts, all our experience of a spiritual world is the one individual, incommunicable *me*; I can only guess that you people have got souls, because you look as if you had and behave as if you had, and the jumbling up of your souls with mine to make a world-soul is an even more difficult thing to imagine than the dissolving of my soul into elements which it hasn't got.

Having told us that, the philosophers go on to prove the doctrine of personal survival from our moral and spiritual experience. That's the only thing which makes you feel as if there must be a catch about it somewhere, because ordinarily one doesn't give two excuses where one will do. But I suppose they feel all this argument about the nature of the soul is rather rarefied, so they go on to other considerations. Kant will tell you that we shouldn't believe in the existence of a just God unless human actions were rewarded and punished hereafter; and other people have refined on that in various ways. If there is really anything Providential in the arrangement of the Universe, is it possible that Man should have been put down here with his appetite for truth and beauty, just allowed to serve a kind of apprenticeship, to flesh his teeth on the half-realized beauties and the half-revealed truths of earth, if there were no fuller satisfaction waiting for him elsewhere, to slake the thirst which his earthly experiences have bred in him? Or alternatively, with a more directly theological appeal, is it possible that Man should have been allowed to discover by hints and half-lights, the existence of a God and of a spiritual order beyond our material horizons, and no chance ever be given him of getting in touch with those truths at first hand? All these are variants of what you may call the bad-luck argument; and if I have had to run through them briefly like that, it is only because my time is at an end, not because I doubt the force of their appeal. They do not, strictly speaking, prove the doctrine of immortality; but they do show reason to think that God must allow us at least a limited period of survival after death—and they would be valid, even if we had no Christian revelation to tell us more.

Only . . . there is a sort of hobgoblin that looks over our shoulders when we are working out all these irrefragable syllogisms, and says, "Yes, but do you really believe that? I mean, are you really prepared to bet on it; not just making a Q.E.D. of it, but a Q.E.F.?" And I am glad there is a Christian revelation to supplement all the encouraging things the philosophers tell us—at least when I wake at four o'clock in the morning.

6

The Necessity of Revelation

I was saying that it ought to be possible, even without any revelation, for a man, and a woolly-headed sort of man at that, to infer the existence of God. And now it looks as if I were trying to persuade you that nobody would believe in God at all if God hadn't seen fit to reveal himself.

Of course, I have stated the contrast rather crudely, but I think it's important to see where we stand. When you are thinking about God, it seems so awful there should be people who don't believe in him that you throw yourself on to that side of the argument; of course God exists; of course you have to admit the difference between right and wrong; of course man has a soul and an immortal destiny. But then you start thinking about Man; you begin to see him in his little-ness, and to be sorry for him; how could a miserable creature like this possibly lift his head out of the slime he wallows in, unless some power from above forced his regard upward? The Fall has disturbed, not only the fixity of his purpose, but the clearness of his vision. You find yourself in the opposite mood, of wondering how it was that the world, before our Lord's coming, had any notion of God at all. Your mind becomes evenly divided, like a College Meeting in which half the dons are saying how monstrous it is that young men should get drunk, and the other half are saying, Yes, but as a matter of fact they do.

What complicates the question, viewed on this level, is that the Church has never quite made up her mind how bad

a crash the Fall was. Oh, I know, you can get an agreed
statement about man being deprived of his supernatural powers and wounded in his natural powers, about the endowments which are owed to his nature and the endowments
which aren't, and all the rest of it. But it remains true that the
general over-all picture of what happened when Adam fell is
seen differently by different theologians. Quite early in
Church history there was a tendency to make light of the
whole thing, and the Pelagians were condemned for talking
as if after all the Fall had made no difference. St Augustine,
reacting from the Pelagian menace, put us all into a very
uncomfortable frame of mind about it. "This was the state of
affairs," he tells us, after the Fall. "The whole human race, a
doomed mass, lay there, wallowing in calamity, went crashing
down from one depth of calamity to the next, enfeoffed to
the party of the apostate angels, and paying the deserved
penalty of its impious rebellion." Well, of course you couldn't
possibly put it fairer than that. But somehow, when you get a
terrific theological statement like that, the human mind won't
remain strung up to concert pitch. You get like Dr Johnson's
friend, who tried to be a philosopher, but cheerfulness would
keep on coming in. The only people who have ever really
tried to put the full Augustinian picture across were the
Jansenists in the seventeenth century. They were reacting
from the humanism which had come in with the Renais-
sance; the rediscovery of the classical authors had made Latin
and Greek antiquity all the rage, and it seemed to the
Jansenists as if we had forgotten that the heathens were
wicked people or ignorant people at all. So you get the Abbé
de St Cyran shaking his head over Virgil, "Poor fellow, to
have written such a lot of fine verse and gone to hell all the
same!" So you get Pascal weighing in with his tremendous
diatribe on the feebleness of man. "Man, then, is no better
than an object full of errors, ineradicable except by grace;
nothing informs him of the truth, everything plays him false."
That was Jansenism, trying to hark back to the early centu-

ries, but they couldn't get away with it; to-day we are in revolt from Jansenism again. So the feelings of the Catholic world oscillate, even when its thought is pegged down by theological definitions.

But they oscillate, as I've tried to indicate, between two poles. We are not concerned, this morning, with the weakening of man's will which the Fall produced, only with the difficulty under which his intellect labors, of finding the truth. We mustn't say, on the one hand that man is incapable of discovering God's existence except by revelation; that is repudiated by the Vatican Council of last century. On the other hand, we mustn't say that his natural reason serves him so well as to make revelation a mere luxury. Why mustn't we? It is a matter of apologetics.

What I am going to argue is that it would be rather bad luck on the human race if there hadn't been a revelation, considering what a poor show we should have put up if we had been left to construct a religion for ourselves. When I use the term "bad luck", I am not speaking theological language. One doesn't claim that God was *bound* to reveal himself; only that we should have expected him to reveal himself, considering how good he is.

Meanwhile, there is another point about which we ought to remind ourselves, a point which Pascal, it seems to me, rather forgot. When we are talking apologetics, we are trying to put the Christian case in such a way that its claims should be evident even to the rationalist. And the rationalist, of course, won't allow us, at this stage of the proceedings, to talk about the Fall. How do we know there ever was any Fall? The fossil apple with the two bites in it has yet to be discovered; we know about the Fall only from revelation, and therefore while we are still laboring to prove the fact of revelation, to base any argument on the Fall would be putting the cart before the horse. No, we must leave the theologians to discuss among themselves the exact extent of human depravity; nothing concerns us here except natural probabilities. What kind of show should we put up, if we had to construct religion for our-selves? And what kind of show has man put up, as a matter of experience, when he has found himself in that position?

As a matter of fact I think the rationalist, being the ratio-nalist he is, would try at this point to stop the whole pro-ceedings. "What's the use", he might argue, "of trying to prove to me that God is *likely* to have revealed himself? If you can prove to me that he *did* reveal himself, then I shall have to believe it, whether it is likely or not. And if you can't prove that he did, then the question of whether he was likely to ceases to be of any interest. After all, there are lots of likely things, aren't there, that come unstuck?" That sounds all right, but I don't think we can let him off. You see, I think he is prejudiced against the proofs of revelation we are going to offer him; he doesn't come to them with an open mind. We shall find him telling us, for example, that he doesn't believe in miracles. But, if he would make his thought coherent, he would find that he really draws the line at divine interference of any kind. Mr Lewis is so good, isn't he, at the beginning of his book on miracles, about the rationalist wanting to inhabit a self-contained world of *na-ture*, ascertainable fact, what he calls "the whole show", out-side which there is nothing. A sealed-off, God-proof little universe, an egg which never hatches, that's what he wants. Any divine interference he resents exactly as a man with a bad cold resents a draught.

Supposing that to-night every Catholic in the world had a dream of our Blessed Lady crowned in heaven. Would that be a miracle? Why, no; not by the definitions. It would only be a breaking of the law of averages, and the law of averages was made to be broken. But your rationalist would hate it; he would at once say that we were all liars, or perhaps that ninety-nine point three recurring of us were liars; it is the divine intrusion he would resent. If a dog got up and made a public speech in the middle of Carfax, it would worry him, but he wouldn't really *mind*, as long as the dog kept off theological topics. As a matter of fact, I understand that the rationalist is already being made to look rather foolish by these tests in the States which seem to demonstrate that a large percentage of the human race can guess the value of a hidden card much oftener than the law of averages would allow for. But it doesn't really worry the rationalist, because, thank goodness, there's none of this religious nonsense about it. It may be preternatural, but it's not supernatural, there is no hen's beak *from the outside* cracking his eggshell.

All that means, that in order to get rid of his *a priori* prejudice we have not merely got to make him allow for the possibility of miracle; we have got to make him allow for any possibility of God, even supposing there is a God, making himself felt, putting his oar in, here in this comfortable world of our common experience. Unfortunately, that prejudice is so deep-seated that we can do very little in the way of combating it. But we can do something, we can do just a little, if we can convince him that there is a real case, here, for divine interference; if we can convince him that man, who was made to be a religious animal, nevertheless cannot function effectively as a religious animal unless and until his natural powers of finding his way to God are supplemented by supernatural means. It doesn't matter at this stage whether it is going to be the Christian revelation, or Moses or Mahomet or Buddha or what you will; the point is that *a* revelation is to be expected. The spiritual blindness of man is not a functional disorder which will yield to time and treatment; it is an organic disease which calls for an operation.

However, it is the Christian revelation we shall, in fact, be concerned with. Now, what is there, or how much is there, in the Christian revelation which we couldn't have got on without? Let us picture ourselves, crudely enough, in the position of the Western European nations, unable to achieve economic recovery without a Marshall plan. "Right," says General Marshall, "how much exactly do you want?" How much ought we to want, as a minimum, in the way of revelation? Because of course Almighty God never goes in for Marshall plans, he always gives us more than we ask for. That is what he is like. Now, take the doctrine of the Blessed Trinity; I don't think any theologian would deny that we could have got on without that. In the sense, I mean, that if God had told us nothing about it, we might have achieved our supernatural end without it. We might have had rather half-baked ideas about the Incarnation, but we could have muddled through somehow. Or take the doctrine that each of us has an angel Guardian; that's a doctrine full of comfort and calculated to make better Christians of us, but once again it's not indispensable. No, these things are extras, thrown in. And there's another point about them—we should never have been able to arrive at the truth of them if they hadn't been revealed to us; no amount of philosophical reasoning would have guaranteed them to us. But, you see, that isn't all revelation does. Besides telling us various things which we didn't know before, and couldn't possibly have known, it also gives us reassurance about certain things which we knew, or half knew, and yet wanted to be reassured about them—heavens, how badly we wanted to be reassured about them!

That there is a God, that right is right and wrong is wrong, we know all that, we can prove all that; and yet the tug of our natures is so strong that we want to be told it over again; we want it shouted at us through a megaphone. Oh, Pascal was right there; the most accomplished mathematician is no better than the rest of us at walking on a plank over a precipice; he *knows* that it is all right, but he can't *feel* that it is all right, with nothing external to himself to support him in the belief. And we, in this tight-rope-walk business of trying to live our lives as if it really mattered, want more than a metaphysical conviction that God exists, want more than an ethical prejudice in favour of right-doing. Our fundamental beliefs, however incontestable they are on paper, have somehow got to be reduced to the scale of actual living, have somehow got to be interwoven with the fabric of our flesh-and-blood experience; we must be able to say, "It happened *then*." We must be able to say, "It happened just *here*." We are creatures of dust, and a memory strikes down to the roots of us more easily than a syllogism.

Even where we have rational certainty, we want to be reassured; these flapping, unmanageable certainties must be pinned down with tent-pegs of fact. And how much more, where we are almost certain but not quite! What I am thinking of is the doctrine of survival after death. I don't know what you feel about it, but I never think the philosophical arguments in its favour are a hundred per cent water-tight; you can disprove the other man's case all right, but can you, with absolute certainty, prove your own? I dare say you can. But just think, how the human mind has been divided over this point, how incessantly it has worried over this point; how, the moment Christian certainty begins to fade, Spiritualism or something of that kind steps in, because we must, somehow, find out. . . . All that doesn't prove that the soul *is* immortal; it might all be wish-thinking, obviously. But, that we should be left without any certainty of whether it is true or not! Does not that state of things *demand* a revelation?

That's the argument. Man troubled with a soul; constitutionally incapable of forgetting God altogether, of stifling conscience altogether, and living contentedly among the beasts; haunted by race-memories of Paradise, and yet equally incapable, when it comes to the point, of sticking to a sane theology, or of living a consistent morality! Now lapsing into silly idolatries, now working himself into a condition of passionate hate at the very mention of the word "God". Now enslaving himself to a set of meaningless taboos, now throwing into some unworthy, some bloodthirsty cause the heroism which should have been devoted to the service of mankind. Is there room, in a rationally governed universe, for the existence of a creature so blinded by the rush-light of his own half-knowledge?

If you would gauge the difference which revelation has
made to our notions of worship, you have only to concentrate on a single *obiter dictum* of Aristotle's. "We should think
it very odd," he says, "to hear anybody talking about loving
Zeus." He is discussing friendship; love is not properly so
called where there is no hope of being loved in return; you
do not, therefore, "love" in the true sense an inanimate object, such as your dinner; nor, for the same reason, a Divine
Being. . . . The exchange of love between God and the individual human soul is to be found, sure enough, in the Old
Testament. A dozen times in Deuteronomy, eight times in
Ecclesiasticus, only thirteen times in the rest of the Old Testament writings. The prophets tell you to fear God, to seek
God, to come back to God, not to love him. Mankind is still
under tutelage. It was not till the full revelation came to us
that we were spoilt with this sense of a Divine intimacy. I use
the word "spoilt" advisedly; for indeed, this sense of intimacy is now something we take for granted. Even your half-
Christianities, which dislike the idea of revelation and will
not tie themselves down with historical assertions, insist
loudly that the love of God is the only thing which matters;
but they are kicking away the ladder they climbed on. It
would not have occurred to them to love God, if something
had not happened in the first century A.D. Revelation, after
all, by the root meaning of it, does not imply that any new
factor has come into force; it draws aside a veil, to let us see a
factor which was there at work all the time. And the really
staggering demand it makes on our powers of belief is when
it assures us that God wants to be loved.

7

Praeparatio Evangelica

On Ash Wednesday morning you indulge in a curious ceremony. You have your faces blacked with ashes, and those ashes have been sprinkled beforehand with lustral water, and had incense waved over them. When I say a curious ceremony I mean a curiously pagan ceremony, in the sense that all the elements of it go right back to the heart of natural religion; the whole business of disguising yourself, trying to obliterate your personality by smearing ashes over your face, would seem at first sight more like the preparation for some savage war-dance in the more primitive parts of Africa than preparation for the Christian Lent. If Virgil walked in in the middle of it, you feel he would say, "What a nice, simple, teaching ceremony!" But of course if a true-blue Protestant walked in he would say nothing of the kind. He would say, "What a revolting throw-back to idolatry!" And it was, if you remember, these rather pagan-looking sacramentals of ours that were first swept away by the Puritans under Edward VI. Candlemas candles and Ash Wednesday ashes and Palm Sunday palms were the very things our medieval forefathers specially loved, perhaps (if the truth must be told) because they had a rather nice pagan feeling about them. So that was the first thing they must learn to do without, in order that they might be transformed into good little Puritans themselves.

There is no sort of doubt that the Church has, and deliberately, retained in her method of worship some of the externals to which the pagan world, which she conquered, had grown accustomed. She incorporated paganism, if I may put it in that way; she didn't abolish it, she swallowed it up. Very much as the *Daily Telegraph* swallowed up the old *Morning Post*. And the Church has tamed and hallowed something of those heathen rites which she dispossessed. Of course that made, and makes, the Puritans terribly angry; they think the Christian religion ought to be something *absolutely* different from all the other religions in the world; to have no leaven of natural religion in it. And all that goes back in the long run to the question whether you think of grace as the old Protestants did, as something which supersedes nature altogether, or think of it as we Catholics do, as something which perfects nature. But we haven't time to talk about that; what I want to suggest to you, in the first half of this conference, is that the findings of natural religion, the instinctive guesses which man makes about Divine things and how Divine things should be approached, weren't wholly wrong. It wasn't a bad shot; it was near enough to the truth to prepare people's minds for the full revelation, when the full revelation came.

If you had a friend, an atheist, who wanted to know what were the characteristic doctrines of Christianity, what marked it out as different from the other religions of the world, to what would you draw attention? The doctrine of the Trinity, probably; and then the Christian belief in the Fall—because oddly enough, although we get the story of the Fall from the Old Testament, the doctrine of it is much more a Christian than a Jewish doctrine. And, as the result of the Fall, man's need of redemption; the fact of sin, the demand for purification from it. And, as meeting that need, as supplying that demand, our Lord's atonement for us on the Cross; our Lord making us mystically one with himself, and so, as our representative, undergoing suffering and public disgrace; strangely enough, having that suffering and that disgrace inflicted on him by the very people who needed, and through his death were achieving, reconciliation with God. And then, as the great central tenet of our creed, the resurrection; a triumph at once over death and over sin by this martyred King of ours, defeat suddenly turned into triumph. With that death and that resurrection, you would say, we are mystically identified when we receive the Sacrament of Baptism; we emerge from a state of enmity with God, or at best from a state of deadness, of neutrality, of nonconductingness, into Life; we are risen creatures, transcending thenceforth the limits which nature imposes on us; ripe for holiness in this life, for a blessed immortality in the next. And most Christians would add, certainly all Catholics would add, that there is a second form of sacramental approach which identifies us with Christ. Only this time it is not a single transaction; it is a frequent and may be a daily action by which we become more and more partakers of his Divine Life, incorporated into him; the Sacrament of the altar. All that, you would say, is the characteristic pattern of the Christian teaching; there are lots and lots of other things one could mention, but there you have the framework of the Christian philosophy.

And of course, if your atheist friend was a really seasoned no-Goddite, he would hoot with laughter. More especially if he happened to have mugged up his brief from Fraser's *Golden Bough* and other anthropological works of that rather dog's-eared school. "Call those the essential doctrines of Christianity if you like," he would say, "call them the most inspiring, the most touching doctrines of Christianity, but don't call them characteristic! That implies that they are the property, the copyright of the Christian religion, that you Christians are the patentees of all these notions about sin and redemption and resurrection and mystical identification and mystical substitution and the rest of it. Instead of which, all these ideas are just pagan ideas, mostly stolen from the mystery religions, which you have dished up so as to look new! Don't you realize that Greek mythology is full of trinities, only they are generally trinities of father, mother and son? Don't you realize that the story of Adam and Eve is just a local Babylonian variant of the myth which accounts for the origin of evil, like the Greek story of Pandora opening Epimetheus' wallet and letting all the plagues in it get loose? And in the same way, that sense of needing redemption, needing purification, was at the root of all the mystery religions; 'I have put evil behind me, and found my way to something better', all that sort of business. Then there is the idea of the king who must be put to death as the representative of his people, publicly, ignominiously—the ancient theologies are full of that; the legend of Pentheus is almost certainly connected with it. The demi-God who rises from the dead is a well-known symbol of the spring and the resurrection of nature with the new crops, you get it everywhere. The whole idea of baptism is the same as that of the Eleusinian mystics rushing down into the sea; the whole idea of assimilating the qualities of a god by partaking in a sacramental meal is much older than Christianity, and survived independently in Mithraism. What you have been giving me as a picture of Christianity in isolation is only a mosaic of bits and pieces picked up from the underworld of paganism, there is nothing new, there is nothing original in it."

Well, of course there's a great deal in Fraser and in Fraser's whole method which is quite obviously bogus; all the evidence is so carefully smoothed away at the edges that the casual reader, quite unable to check his author's facts, will sit there open-mouthed in astonishment, but it's a sell really. But in so far as these resemblances exist, and they obviously do, what are we to make of them? The notion that Christianity is a synthetic religion which deliberately borrowed these elements from paganism simply won't do, because these elements demonstrably go back to the preaching of our Lord himself, and our Lord demonstrably wasn't the kind of person who would, or humanly speaking could, build up a synthetic religion from such models. Are we to say, then, that the resemblances are a mere fluke? Well, you know, it may be so. The human mind is extraordinarily infertile of ideas. When people sit down to invent stories, whether they are

primitive witch-doctors or modern novelists, it is extraordinary how few plots there really are to choose from. Andrew
Lang pointed out that the whole business of Ulysses giving
his name to Polyphemus as Nobody, so that when the other
Cyclops people asked, "Who is attacking you?" Polyphemus
should reply, "Nobody is attacking me"—all that occurs just
the same in a Norse saga which couldn't possibly have been
copied from the *Odyssey*, or the *Odyssey* from it. And if you
like, you can accept all the resemblances between paganism
and Christianity with a shrug of the shoulders, and say, "So
what?"

But I confess it seems to me a more natural solution of the
problem to say that Divine Providence encouraged the human mind to develop these myths, these fantasies, these
mumbo-jumbo ceremonies, precisely so that the human
mind might be ready for the true revelation when the true
revelation came. Why do the birds make nests just when they
are going to lay eggs? You don't know, nor do I, nor does
anybody; but it is a great convenience that the eggs shouldn't
have to be rolling about on the ground. So, it seems to me,
Almighty God didn't want his revelation to reach the human
mind as something quite strange, quite foreign to all its ways
of thought, difficult to assimilate. He would shape the human mind beforehand to receive it, as the bird, under some
strange tuition of instinct, shapes the nest beforehand to suit
its unimagined needs.

All that would be arresting enough; but of course it's only
half the story—less than half. At the same moment when he
was preparing the Gentile world, all unconscious of what it
meant, for the coming of the Christ, he was preparing the
Jewish world for the coming of the Christ, half-conscious,
but only *half*-conscious, of what it meant. I've been wallowing in the Old Testament for the last two years or more, as
few people are ever in a position to wallow in it, and I simply
can't get over the extraordinariness of the Jewish people. I
mean, even if you approach the Old Testament without any

belief in inspiration, without any prejudice in favor of its accuracy, there is something obstinately Providential about the story of the Jews. Even if Christianity had never happened, it would still challenge belief, the way in which this tiny nation has drawn a trail of theology over the face of history; the way in which all its literature, and such superb literature, reduces itself to an epic of the soul. Let me rough out for you the lines of that epic, in very brief form.

Here is a people closely allied, by race and language, to all the neighbouring peoples; quite inexplicably—we won't quarrel about the date, there is no questioning the fact—it goes monotheist. It is no longer content to boast of its God Yahweh as superior to the neighbouring tribal gods, as a better option than Moloch, as a slight advance on Chemosh; its tribal God is proclaimed as the only real God; the rest are all fairy-stories. That was not the result of some geographical accident; curiously, it was when they were in exile that the Jews were most certain of their odd conviction, in their own country that they were most liable to slip back into heathen ways. They followed up this strange notion with a still stranger taboo; their God must not be represented by any images; in theory, and later in practice, he was to have only one shrine, the temple precincts at Jerusalem. A further point; this God, although he was the universal ruler of the world, was conceived as bound to them, the people of the Jews, by a special treaty relationship. He would support their cause among the nations so long, and only so long, as they honoured certain obligations on their side. The list of these obligations was called the law, and the punctilious observance of the law was described by the word which is, rather misleadingly, translated in our Bibles as "justice". It's a great mistake to think of the Mosaic law as if it was wholly, or even as if it was chiefly, concerned with morals. Where the word "sin" is used in the law it nearly always means a stupid oversight, like eating a mutton chop on Friday when you've forgotten that it is a Friday, which is not what we mean by sin at all. Huge sections of the Law are about being very careful to wear tassels on the fringes of your garments, and not to eat seagulls. But somehow, built into the structure of this elaborate code of ritual and of manners, you find a moral code that is fully satisfying to our best ethical ideas, that is often curiously exacting. Among other things it is specially designed to prevent anybody being too fond of money, and consequently of driving a hard bargain. Somehow, in fact, the kind of religion which Greek philosophy only dreamed of, only dreamed of in its most enlightened moments, grew up apparently self-sown among one particular Semitic tribe, not in any way distinguished from the other Semitic tribes by its general level of culture. The one God, the God who is so spiritual a being that you must not represent him even by a human figure, the God who demands, as the price of his favour, kindliness to the poor, honesty in all your dealings, the avoidance, at least, of gross sensual excess—all that, the dream of the sage, is the common birthright of Israel.

Then there's another extraordinary thing about this extraordinary people; I have tried to express it somewhere by saying that the Jewish nation moves backwards through history. The Jews were always looking forward to a good time coming later on. In all their fiercest afflictions, they only grew more confident of this apparently forlorn hope; one day, the Messias would come, and then it would be all right. Already, as the epistle to the Hebrews points out, Abraham and his immediate descendants had lived in hope, waiting for the fulfillment of a Divine promise. Moses, in a single phrase which was still remembered a thousand years afterward, had foretold that God would raise up a second Prophet like himself. But it was with the dynasty of King David—take it all in all, not a very interesting or a very impressive dynasty—that this unconquerable hope in the future grew up. And it triumphed over exile.

It did more than triumph over exile; exile purified it, rarefied it, extended the scope of it. The great tradition of the prophets taught Israel to give a new direction to this hope, and a distinctively moral one. Israel had sinned, that was why Israel had fallen into captivity. And it would be the business of the Christ, the Messias, when he came, not only to deliver his people from oppression, but to deliver them from their sins. Not all of them; it would be a remnant of the Jews, the obedient Jews, the patient Jews, that would be the citizens of his kingdom. And meanwhile, the person of the Christ who was to come began to take shape in the mists of prophetic vision. If he was to take away sins, he must be a victim for sins, like the sheep that were slaughtered in the ritual of temple sacrifice. On the other hand, could a merely human Messias, fallible like the rest of us, be adequate to the rôle of a world-ruler, as that rôle was now conceived? Must he not rather prove a supernatural Being, a son of God in some mysterious sense which made it safer to refer to him as the Son of Man? It was this latter notion of "him who was to come" that chiefly gained ground in the five centuries before our era; it owed its popularity in the main to the prophecy of Daniel. And for some reason it seems quite clear that the coming of the Messias was actually dated by Daniel's prophecy; dated to happen at about the time when our Lord actually came. No intelligible account can be given of the gospel narrative until you recognize that.

I haven't spoken at all of the external preparation for our Lord's coming, remarkable as it was. I mean, the Providential direction of the world-order, which decreed that when he came the whole of the known world should have been civilized by a veneer at least of Hellenism; that the Greek language should be, to a degree unique in history, a *lingua franca* all over the East, that Roman conquests should have pacified the nations, Roman roads should have made travel and communication easy; that the all-important Jewish race should have been scattered everywhere, so that the missionaries of the new faith always found a synagogue as their lever for starting work. I have only spoken of the preparation in men's minds. In men's minds, could any more elaborate nest have been built in readiness for the coming of the Dove at Pentecost?

8

The Messianic Hope

The Jewish people is one of the most extraordinary facts in history. Pascal was right about that; you mustn't attempt any Christian apologetic which would by-pass or hush up the connexion of Christianity with Judaism; it's all part of the set-up. And one of the extraordinary things about the Jewish people is this—it dreams of the future, not of the past. The Jew is always looking forward to a good time coming, instead of lamenting the good old times which will never come again. Nowadays, we don't find that surprising, because for nearly two centuries we have been obsessed with the idea of human progress; and even in our own alarmingly regressive age we can't, or at any rate we older people can't, shake off the spell of it. But remember, this has only been happening for two centuries, since some priest or other, I forget his name, invented the idea of human progress. The primitive instinct of man, everywhere else, is to look back to the past and regret its disappearance. Diomede in Homer picks up a stone and hurls it at his enemy, a stone which would take three men to lift it, says the poet, the sort of men there are going about nowadays, but Diomede managed it easily alone. The golden age of Saturn—from the very beginnings of Gentile literature you find this hankering for the past; men only took to writing, it would seem, when the world already felt that it had grown old. But that is not the note of Hebrew literature, and remember what a bulk of Hebrew literature has come down to us. There are appeals to God's ancient

72

mercies; there are tall stories about the exploits of David and his mighty men. But the note of Hebrew literature is optimism about the future. The Jew had his story of a lost Paradise, just as the heathen had theirs, but he hardly ever referred to it; the Fall just disappears from the Old Testament after the third chapter of Genesis. It wasn't Adam's fall that was remembered; it was the promises made to Abraham.

Well, what about Abraham? We can't prove, of course, the antiquity of the records which have come down to us; but he is in the very centre of a living tradition which always tells the same story. He was only a desert sheikh, perhaps a little richer in flocks and herds than his neighbours, but, to all outward appearance, very much out of the same drawer. This only would have struck you about him as distinguishing him from the rest; he seemed to live in the future. "In thy seed," he had been told, "all the nations of the earth shall be blessed"—that may only mean, "Your descendants will be so prosperous that they will be quoted, everywhere, as typical of a successful career; *May you be as prosperous as the sons of Abraham* will be a kind of proverbial saying." But in any case he seems to have had the conviction that his family possessed a unique importance; and if it was a personal kink, it was one which he handed on to his posterity. When Jacob went into Egypt, he was far better off than he had ever been in Chanaan. But when he dies, he makes his children swear that his bones shall be taken back to the country of his birth. To him, already Chanaan was the holy land; he must not be buried anywhere else; that parched strip of Levantine coast was to have an importance of its own, some day.

The Exodus from Egypt is not the common story of a nation which has grown too big, swarming like a hive of bees until it has found somewhere else to settle down. It is represented consistently as a return to the country in which Abraham and the other patriarchs had lived. Not that we should attach any importance to that very misleading word "inheritance" which our versions use, quite wrongly, as a description of Chanaan. The Israelites did not inherit Palestine from Abraham, it had never belonged to him. No, the sense in which the word is used is that of an allotted territory; Providence had arranged that this particular people and this particular country should belong to one another, and in perpetuity. The return from Egypt (always thought of as a return) became a pattern in the minds of the Jewish people, a pattern which would repeat itself at intervals; drive out the Jews from Palestine as much as you would, sooner or later they were destined to return. It is a notion which has even influenced Christian speculation; there was an ingenious clergyman in the eighteenth century who considered the question why the rivers of America all flow from west to east, and concluded that it was meant to facilitate the return of the Jews to Palestine at the end of the world. How deeply that confidence has sunk into the Jewish mind, the events of our own day bear witness. Meanwhile the great hero of the Exodus, Moses, had foretold quite casually, in an unimportant context, that God would one day raise up a prophet like himself. Astonishingly, that *obiter dictum* was remembered twelve and a half centuries later; the first question that rose to men's lips when they tried to solve the mystery of John the Baptist was "Art thou the Prophet?"

The institution of monarchy seems to have been a late, and, on the whole, an unpopular expedient where the Jewish people was concerned. The hereditary principle was even less securely established; Saul, the great hero of national resistance to the Philistines, left no effective dynasty behind him, and the crown went to David, as we know. And now comes the extraordinary thing, this interloper, this *arriviste*, the first king of his line, immediately proceeds to found a literary legend about the unalterable permanence of his own dynasty. Whichever of the psalms King David did or didn't write, you can see that they are all in a single literary tradition, and here is this legend of an immortal Davidic dynasty fairly let into the middle of it. It is exactly as if all the Scottish songs about

Prince Charlie had been written about Richard Cromwell. Thenceforward, a fresh element entered into the Messianic hope. The Jewish race believed, not merely that God would bring them back home again when they went into exile, but that he would restore their country as a monarchy under a descendant of King David.

So you get on to the age of the prophets. Why do we use the word prophet, in our common speech, to designate somebody who can foresee the future? A prophet doesn't mean that; he is simply a spokesman, usually the spokesman of a God. The reason why we think of a prophet as a man who foretells the future is because the spokesman of God, in the Old Testament, foretold the future. The unconquerable Jewish instinct of looking forward has left its mark, here, on the vocabulary of the human race. The Old Testament prophets lived at a time when the captivity in Babylon was impending, and while it was happening, and just after it came to an end; their message is mixed up, from first to last, with visions of the future, calculated to bring warning or comfort to their fellow countrymen in those days of uncertainty. And although, taken one by one, those visions of the future were and are tantalizingly obscure, you could make up a sort of composite picture out of them—which is what the Jews did. By the time our Lord came, you can see that they had in their minds a fairly definite programme of what the Messias was expected to do, and what his kingdom was to be like. For some reason—I think it was connected with the dates suggested in the prophecy of Daniel, but that is guesswork—the Jews of our Lord's time were expecting the Messianic kingdom to come at any moment. You see them, all through the gospels, keyed up with expectation, from old Simeon in the temple, waiting for comfort to be brought to Israel, right down to that scene just before the Ascension, when the Apostles ask our Lord whether he is going to restore the kingdom to Israel immediately or not; they are still, you see, talking the language of Old Testament prophecy.

Of course, any nation which has suffered defeat and exile has its own dreams of a happier time to come, when its liberties will be restored. But the Messianic hope went further than that; it wasn't simply that the Jews would regain their independence from the Babylonians or the Persians or the Seleucids or the Romans or whoever happened to be top dog just then. There was going to be a new world-order, in which Providence visibly interfered to make things go right instead of wrong; universal peace, universal justice. To be sure, the Jewish nation was going to have a privileged place in this new world-order; Jerusalem would be the capital of it, as the son of David would be the reigning monarch of it. But the Gentiles were going to have a look-in, and that was already something, when you remember how the Jews regarded their neighbours. Meanwhile, this new kingdom would be ushered in by a time of general distress and disaster; and it would not be the whole Jewish people, but a remnant of the Jewish people, that would live to triumph. There could be no Messianic kingdom without a moral regeneration. The Jewish people had sinned, had oppressed the poor and gone after false gods; that was why their enemies always harassed and finally defeated them. It would be the business of the Messias to deliver them, not merely from their enemies, but from their sins.

All this can't be simply pushed on one side as being part of the Old Testament, and consequently boring. It is built right into the fabric of revelation; the Evangelists are continually conscious of our Lord's career as tracing in the lines of a blue-print which has been laid down for him by the prophets—what other book is there in the world which gives you the sense of fulfillment as the gospels do? Where else do you get the impression that the chief business of history is to make prophecy come true? . . . You see, all that old-fashioned Victorian business of reading the gospels as the story of a good man who was misunderstood by his contemporaries—it just isn't historical. Before you try to discover whether and in what sense our Lord was Divine, before you try to discover what is meant by the title "Son of God", you have to ask yourself the question, "Was Jesus of Nazareth, or was he not, the Messianic king Isaias and those others referred to?" Because that was the claim which he made; that was the question which puzzled his friends, and the question which puzzled his enemies.

I was reminding you just now that the Pharisees asked St John the Baptist, "Art thou the prophet?"—in reference to the promise made by Moses that a second prophet, like Moses himself, would one day appear. The Pharisees never seem to have asked our Lord that question; I wonder why not? I think because he so obviously *did* claim to be the prophet in question; he was always saying "Moses told you this, but *I* tell you this"; when he published the programme of his new kingdom he went up on to a mountainside to do it, just like Moses, and when he fed the Five Thousand he was thinking—St John shows you that—of the manna in the wilderness. If he claimed to be the prophet, did he also claim to be the Messianic king? You can see that he did; people cried out to him as the Son of David, and he never rebuked them for it. As if to make it quite clear that he did put forward this claim, he went out of his way to ride into Jerusalem on an ass; it wasn't a coincidence, it wasn't a Providential arrangement, it was a quite deliberate gesture on his part to make the prophecy come true.

And it isn't difficult to see what must have puzzled the men of his time about all this. By his account of it, the King had come and the kingdom hadn't. Their reading of the prophets encouraged them to expect a Day of the Lord, a general show-down following on a general world-upheaval; one like the Son of Man would come on the clouds, and arraign the nations before his judgement-seat. Instead of that, one who called himself the Son of Man walked about the earth just like anybody else, and nothing happened. That was the sense of John the Baptist's question, "Is it thy coming that

was told, or are we still waiting for some other?" That is why
the two disciples on the road to Emmaus talk so despon-
dently about the Crucifixion; "For ourselves, we had hoped
that it was he who was to deliver Israel; but now, to crown it
all, to-day is the third day since this befell." They have heard
rumors of the Resurrection, but that, evidently, was not what
they were waiting for; they were waiting for "the redemption
of Israel", a Day of the Lord which would put everything
right. And it was the same with our Lord's enemies; when
they asked for a sign they weren't simply asking for a
miracle—there were plenty of them; they were wanting the
sign of the Son of Man, made visible in judgement. And
when, in the Council chamber, he is challenged to say
whether he is really the Christ, he anticipates that objection.
"I am," he says; "and moreover I tell you this; you will see
the Son of Man again, when he . . . comes on the clouds of
heaven"—you will see him like that at some future time, not
now; you mustn't expect to see it now. It was as a king
without a kingdom that our Lord was condemned.

We all know what account he himself gave of it. The
kingdom of heaven, he explained, is something that comes
unwatched by men's eyes; it grows like the seed in the field,
radiates its influence like leaven in the bread; it is a secret, not
a sudden process, the coming of the Son of Man. The kingdom of heaven is not a millennium on earth, with all wrongs
put right; there will be tares left to grow among the wheat; it
will not be till the harvest that the weeds are pulled up, not
till the end of the day that the fishermen will sort out their
catch. A kingdom, but not ruled over visibly by him who is
king of it, he will have gone away into a far country, leaving
his servants to get on as best they can without him. And so
on; he makes it clear, at the same time, that it will not be a
kingdom for the Jews only; a remnant of them will take their
places in it, but only a remnant, as Isaias foretold; many will
be called, but few chosen. The Gentiles, instead of being left
out in the cold, will enjoy the privileges of this kingdom to

the full. We, with the long history that lies behind us, have no difficulty at all in recognizing this as a portrait of the universal Church, and in identifying the Church with the kingdom he came to found. The only difficulty we sometimes feel is how we are going to make it square with the Old Testament. Was it really this sort of thing the prophets meant, when they sketched their picture of a triumphant Israel, vindicated at last from its enemies and recognized as God's people?

I believe the answer to that difficulty is that we don't know what God would have done for his ancient people if they had accepted, instead of refusing, the Christ. You've only to read St Paul's epistle to the Romans to realize how puzzled the early Christians were to find the Jews persisting in their unbelief. That went on, I think, right up to the time when Jerusalem was destroyed in A.D. 70; that tragic moment in history which looked as if it were going to be the fulfillment of the Old Testament prophecies, and wasn't. Prophecies can be conditional; and we have no means of knowing what mercies God had for his ancient people, or what part he meant them to play in the religious history of the world, if Jerusalem had known the time of her visitation.

Meanwhile, in rejecting our Lord, they fulfilled the Old Testament prophecies to the letter. I think it is Pascal who makes such a strong point of that; all that passage at the end of Isaias, about the suffering servant of God, bruised for his people's sins while they turned away their faces from him and thought he was smitten by God, all that was meant, surely, to prepare us for what actually happened. And our Lord knew that it would happen, and modelled his Messianic career on these other, these less-known prophesies, which had fallen into neglect. That is what makes the argument from prophecy so splendid, if you know your Old Testament a little; that our Lord is carefully and consciously tracing out the blueprint of prophecy just when it looks as if he were getting it all wrong. Just when we want to pull him up, as St Peter did, and tell him he is going about the thing in the wrong way, he knows his business better than we do, and sees the whole picture of the Messias when we only see a part of it. We mustn't think of the Old Testament as an awkward fact which we've got to get over somehow, hush it up if possible because it is so difficult to make propaganda out of it. It's the lock into which the key of the Incarnation fits, and if you begin the Bible with St Matthew, it makes a mutilated story.

9

The New Testament

I ought to warn you that I am trying to do something which is, I will not say impossible, but essentially unreal. My job is to try and convince you that the New Testament record is a genuine record, without discussing the contents of that record. That is the way, you see, theologians like to go to work; they will find out whether the gospels are accurate accounts of fact, prescinding from what the gospels say. (A really seasoned theologian spends most of his life prescinding from things.) But of course that is not in fact the way in which any human mind works. We pick up, say, a pamphlet about the situation in Greece, and all the time we are reading it we are juggling in our minds with two separate questions, (i) What is really happening in Greece? and (ii) Does this man tell the truth? We are all the time balancing one possibility against another. And so is the ordinary man, not yet a Christian, if you get him to read the New Testament. The way one has to treat the thing in apologetics, first of all proving the gospels are genuine, and then saying to ourselves, Therefore such and such statements, being in the gospels, must be all right, is rather like a slow-motion picture of a man cracking a whip. It's not impossible, but it's unreal.

First, though, let's just mention how our Christian documents stand merely as documents. We have full manuscripts of the New Testament which go back to the fourth century, whereas our oldest MS of Tacitus, for example, about the same period of writing, only dates from the ninth century.

There were five centuries during which anybody so disposed may have been faking the manuscripts of Tacitus, but during those centuries nobody tampered with our documents—we have the documents themselves to prove it. Not to mention the earlier fragments of papyrus, which go very much further back. And in all the vast mass of written copies we possess, the differences are (you may say) infinitesimal; only now and again do you wish that scribes had been more careful. And then behind all that you've got the vast amount of quotations in the Fathers which quote manifestly from these same documents which we've got, and tell you which of them were regarded from the earliest times as authentic. I don't mean that there aren't slight hesitations about all this; you can't prove who wrote the epistle to the Hebrews, and you can't prove that the Apocalypse was universally recognized from the earliest times as being an apostolic document. But you can build up, on critical principles, a sufficient scaffolding of knowledge about what Christians believed in the middle of the first century to make all our other knowledge of such remote times look silly by comparison. Imagine if we knew as much about the life of Socrates as we do about the life of Christ, if we knew as much about the worship of Mithras as we do about the worship of Christ!

But all that, which is very important, is too big a claim to implement in a conference of this length. What I want to do is rather to examine the records themselves, as literature, and suggest to you the remarkable absence of anything that could be called phoney about them. First of all, let's leave the gospels out of account altogether. The rest of the New Testament, if you come to think of it, would give us the whole of the Apostles' Creed, except the two clauses "conceived by the Holy Spirit, born of the Virgin Mary"; and even so it would leave us wondering where all this very unJewish admiration for virginity had sprung up from. Or, for the moment, let's cut down the area of our observation even more closely; look simply at the Acts of the Apostles and the letters of St

Paul. You have still got the whole of the Apostles' Creed there. Now, the man who wrote the Acts of the Apostles either did know St Paul's letters or he didn't. If he did, and if he was just making up the story as he went along, how remarkable that he should have missed the obvious opportunities of making his account fit in with St Paul's! St Paul says he was shipwrecked three times, St Luke only mentions one shipwreck, and that long after the ones referred to. St Paul says he was beaten five times by the Jews, St Luke doesn't mention any of them. St Paul says he went off into Arabia, for a kind of retreat, I suppose, after his conversion; St Luke doesn't seem to have heard of it. And so it is all through; the two accounts never dove-tail suspiciously well. On the other hand, if he didn't know St Paul's epistles, didn't know anything about St Paul much, but was merely inventing a biography, how did he get him so right? Not merely the facts of his life or the places he went to, but the man himself, his atmosphere. St Paul's quick temper, when he calls the high priest a whited wall, and his quick recoil, "I'm sorry, I never realized it was the high priest." St Paul's manipulation of pathos—telling the elders of Ephesus they would see his face no more; they did, of course, but they might not have. St Paul's anxiety to avoid scandal, having St Timothy circumcised, and so on; St Paul being all things to all men, getting the Pharisees on his side in the Sanhedrin by announcing that he is being persecuted because he believes in the resurrection of the dead; St Paul ready at a pinch to stick up for his rights, because after all if any is bold, he is bold also—scourge him? he is a Roman citizen; deny him justice? he appeals to Caesar. All the background of St Paul's mind is there in the Acts, in the most extraordinary way; you simply couldn't have invented it.

There's lots more you could say about St Luke; he was a man, I think, with a morbidly accurate mind, hardly less so than Sir William Ramsay's, and you will have to go to the works of Sir William Ramsay if you want to understand what a morbidly accurate mind St Luke had. But we must go on to St Paul's epistles themselves. Do you ever notice one curious difference about the letters one gets; some of your correspondents have the knack of writing as if there were nobody else in the room but you two, and others write as if there was an audience, or as if they expected their letter to be published in *The Times* next day? Most of the letters preserved to us from antiquity are of the latter kind; Cicero is occasionally confidential, but not often, the younger Pliny simply sticks down what he thinks his biographer would like him to stick down, for all the world like a Victorian aunt. But St Paul—what a difference! He writes exactly what he feels, leaves it entirely to the Holy Spirit to do the inspiration; argues, challenges, reproaches, weeps, rants, boasts with every changing mood that passes over him. You must know what it is to be in the room when your hostess is having one of those conversations on the telephone after seven o'clock, when you don't even know who the person at the other end is, let alone what he or she is saying. A great deal of it is all meaningless to you, but every now and then some piece of information emerges which you had no idea of; you gather that your hostess's husband has been knighted, or that she is just bringing out a book on fossils, or that it's her birthday to-day—something of that sort. Well, the theology of St Paul leaks out rather like that. He doesn't sit down to write a dogmatic treatise. He is dealing with some actual situation, some very live situation; and what often makes it so difficult to understand him is that we don't know what the person at the other end of the wire has been saying. But incidentally, quite incidentally, St Paul's highly elaborated system of theology leaks out.

It's so with his theology of the Trinity; he never sat down to tell anybody what they ought to believe about the Holy Trinity, but he keeps on working in threefold formulas about Almighty God which show you that it was at the back of his mind all the time. It's so with his theology of baptism; they knew all about it already, but his presentation of the doctrine, a very characteristic one, keeps on betraying itself in casual allusions. Even the evidence for the Resurrection only comes in because some people at Corinth had started doubting the Resurrection; even his recital of the words of Institution only come in because some people at Corinth were being disrespectful to the Holy Eucharist. You see, then, what I mean about St Paul's letters; they are genuine documents. Just at the end of his life the pastoral epistles wear rather more the air of being manifestoes; and the epistle to the Hebrews isn't really a letter at all, it's a sort of prize essay got up to look as if it were a letter. But in all that earlier correspondence of his you feel the actualities of the situation tingling in every line he writes. They are authentic, not merely in the sense that they were written in the first century, not merely in the sense that it was St Paul who wrote them. They are authentic letters in the sense that he wasn't writing for effect, he was simply sticking down what came into his head. And when a person writes like that you can find out what he really believes, what are the real commonplaces of his thought.

I think with your permission we will leave out the letters written by the other Apostles, and the Apocalypse. Not because one can't argue strongly in favour of their genuineness, but because, with the incomplete picture we've got both of the writers and of the people they are writing to, we can't be sure that they have this splendid spontaneity which is the hallmark of St Paul's writings. And we have a good deal of ground still to cover in discussing the authenticity of the gospels.

One thing is quite evident about the Gospel record—all that I have been saying about St Paul does *not* apply to it. In St Paul you have an obvious unity of authorship; untidy as his epistles are, nobody has ever tried to cut them up into strips. Whereas the first three gospels, if I may say so, fall apart as soon as you look at them; almost every paragraph invites the eager critic to start discussing the source it came from. In St Paul you have the imprint of a vigorous, living personality;

whereas only one of the Evangelists, the fourth, has really marked characteristics, and those almost too much so—you are often at a loss to know where it is that our Lord stops speaking and St John begins. St Paul gives you your lessons in theology absent-mindedly, in the course of talking about something else; the Evangelists are writing with an express purpose, with a definite story to tell. And I think really one of the chief reasons which makes it difficult for people who have not been effectively under Christian influence when they were young to turn to the gospels and give the whole Christian message a candid consideration, is that they are held up by all the fuss and bother there has been and is about the Synoptic problem, and the criticism of the fourth gospel. You would have to read such libraries of books before you felt you had sufficiently considered the value of your sources; and all that only as a preface to the process of finding out what it is your sources have to tell you!

After all, two hundred years ago, in John Wesley's time, if a man wanted to look into the truth of Christianity, he was invited to inspect the four gospels as four quite independent documents, telling the same story each in its own way. You have here (he was told) two eyewitnesses of what happened, Matthew and John, recounting what they saw. You have Mark, the interpreter of Peter, giving Peter's evidence at second hand; you have Luke, with his acute historian's mind, putting together the evidence he had derived from various sources. Often they cover the same bit of ground, but always with just that variety of detail which proves their independence without leaving us in any doubt about what really happened. Well, the whole thing has changed since scholars took to putting on two pairs of spectacles and watching every word as it comes. Most of them have been schoolmasters in their time, and the first thing a schoolmaster has to learn is to spot where boys have been cribbing. And the Holy Evangelists evidently have been cribbing; there is enough detailed resemblance about them to make a clear case for sending up to the headmaster. Did they copy one another, or did they make use of the same document, or documents, now lost? Probably the latter. Anyhow the enquirer, with the furrowed brow of the schoolmaster who finds out that there has been cribbing in his form, tends to ask, "In that case, how can one be certain of anything?"

Well, you know, I don't think it's as bad as all that. The learned people, with the best will in the world, have made it all seem unnecessarily difficult by inventing so many different theories about the precise *way* in which the thing was done. But the broad facts emerge without much difficulty; that there must have been a standard tradition about our Lord's life (whether committed to writing or handed on by word of mouth doesn't make much difference) which the first three Evangelists used, all of them, as the skeleton round which their narrative was to be built. In great part, it seems to have consisted of reported utterances of our Lord, parables and so on. Besides this, each of the three men obviously would have and obviously did have access to a certain amount of independent tradition, out of which he supplied flesh and nerves to his skeleton. Sometimes this independent tradition would overlap so far as its contents were concerned, but untidily and at haphazard, as you can see in the narratives of the Resurrection. Now, the question is, Doesn't all that rather suggest hanky-panky? I mean, that we have only got the evidence of authors who went on hearsay; if they had been eyewitnesses of the events, would they have had to depend on documents? And we can't really get back, now, to the absolute sources; find out what these stories actually said, when they were fresh from the mint.

I don't know. Put it in this way; we are not to think of the twelve Apostles as a set of reporters at a conference, each of them eager to get to the telephone first and put his story through. Think, rather, of some meal you have taken with some religious community, and how they sat round afterwards and told stories of old Father So-and-so, now dead; how some of the stories, to the community, were chestnuts, and there were others which the young ones hadn't heard before. That is the sort of atmosphere in which stories of the Founder are cradled. I once heard Cardinal Bourne say that he had talked with old members of the Salesian community—he knew Don Bosco himself—and these people used to tell him that in the early days at Turin miracles were so common that you hardly talked about them. I don't mean you could canonize a saint on that sort of evidence; I'm only trying to give you the atmosphere. The Gospel as preached by the Apostles was a very brief outline; you get it in the Acts, you get it in First Corinthians. But, as they met day after day, of course the Apostles talked over old times and exchanged memories of what our Lord did and said—especially of what he said, because we are all apt to forget conversations. And thus there grew up a set of reminiscences—I would call them a set of chestnuts if the phrase weren't too irreverent—which had been told over and over again. And not on that account— heaven help these critics!—losing anything in the way of accuracy. On the contrary, *gaining* in accuracy, because one man is correcting his memories with the help of the man next door. By the time the Apostles separated, whenever that was, this body of reminiscences had automatically acquired a fixed content, but with no definite shape, because it was the spontaneous outcome of casual conversations. Perhaps it was written down, but there was no need for it to be written down. Any Apostle would give you the same version, because they had thrashed it out so often. Nobody would set out to write a life of our Lord unless he was either, like St Matthew, a member of the privileged circle, or, like Mark or Luke, had access to a member of it. Naturally, the man who had access to this common tradition wouldn't feel bound to put it all down; every historian selects. St Matthew wouldn't bother his Palestinian readers with the long account you get in St Mark—if that did belong to the common tradition—about the death of St John the Baptist; it would be all Queen Anne to them. St Luke, writing for Gentiles, might think it was all rather off the point. St Mark and St Luke, writing in Rome, might easily leave out the *Tu es Petrus* on the ground that the Bishop of Rome was in danger enough as it was, without putting ideas into people's heads; the leader of the underground movement may prefer to remain anonymous. But the skeleton would be the same.

Why didn't that happen over the story of the Resurrection? I think because each Evangelist wanted, there, to tell the story he got from his private sources; the common tradition, you can see from St Paul, was well known enough. But the private traditions weren't, for that reason, of doubtful authority; it simply happened that they didn't figure in the gossip of the Cenacle. Meanwhile, notice this. With all the libraries that have been written about the Synoptic problem, I have never heard of any critic who tried to show that the general picture given of Jesus Christ in these private sources was different from that given in the common source. Isn't that rather remarkable, except on the assumption that in outline, at any rate, the whole thing is genuine?

I haven't left myself any time to talk about St John's gospel. I always feel there is a riddle in it which some day somebody will solve. I hope one of you will. Meanwhile, it is best to keep clear of St John when you are dealing with a person who doesn't accept the Christian revelation as a fact. There are too many loop-holes for him; he can always quote learned precedent for questioning its date, its authorship, its accuracy.

That's a horribly sketchy conference. And what you are all wanting to say is, Yes, but is it true? I can't give you, in this conference, the answer to that. As I say, you can't discuss whether a document is true without discussing what it says. All I have been trying to point out is that it rings true. The documents of the New Testament are documents that belong to real life, not an elaborate literary fraud. Read the epistles of St Ignatius of Antioch, read any of the apocryphal gospels, and I think you will see what I mean.

10

The Christology of St Paul

If all the documents of the New Testament were lost, except the epistles of St Paul, what should we know about the human life of Jesus of Nazareth?

Roughly, this. That he was born the son of a Jewish woman, descended from King David, but in humble circumstances. That he went through all the trials of human experience, but never committed sin. That his teaching forbade the remarriage of divorced persons. That his Divine mission was attested by power, *dunamis*, which regularly means in St Paul miraculous action. That he instituted a Sacrament, in which his Body and Blood were received under the forms of bread and wine. That his life was a sacrifice of obedience, perfected by submitting to a shameful death from which he had prayed to be delivered. That he bore witness to the convictions by which he lived, in an interview with Pontius Pilate. That he died by crucifixion, rose again from the dead on the third day, and appeared to many of his followers who could attest the fact. That all this was recent history when St Paul wrote; Jesus had a brother, or rather a cousin, with whom St Paul had conversed at Jerusalem. That, and nothing more.

The immediate importance of all this, when we are talking about apologetics, is that the witness of St Paul is quite a separate thing from the witness of the gospels; it is a separate strand in the rope which ties us to the certainties of the faith. After all, get anybody in the world who has heard of Jesus Christ to give you an account, nowadays, of what Jesus Christ was, and you will certainly be told that Jesus Christ went about the world doing good, healing the sick and giving sight to the blind, and so on. There is no word of all that in St Paul. And yet think how natural it would have been for him, as it is for us, to hold up Jesus Christ as a pattern of self-denial and generosity and untiring energy! But no; he tells the Corinthians to follow his example, as he follows the example of Christ; imagine a modern preacher doing that! He tells the Philippians to be humble, but the model of humility he proposes to them is not Jesus Christ's behaviour when he lived in the world incarnate, but Jesus Christ's condescension in becoming incarnate at all. Always he misses the opportunity of telling us a story, the story of the greatest Man who ever lived.

And again, think how much space is occupied in all the gospels by long extracts from what our Lord *said*. Very probably, even before the gospels were written, there were collections of these sayings passing from hand to hand. But St Paul only once quotes a piece of moral teaching given by our Lord, and that is the phrase, "It is more blessed to give than to receive", a phrase which doesn't come in the gospels at all. Yet think how much of our Lord's teaching was devoted to showing the Jews that they could no longer claim a monopoly of the Divine mercies, they had got to shove up and make room for the Gentiles in the Church as well; parables like that of the Labourers in the Vineyard or that of the Prodigal Son! All that was a subject on which St Paul felt and wrote furiously; all through the Galatians and the Romans he is talking about nothing else. But he never quotes our Lord as having said anything on the subject, never borrows an illustration, even, from our Lord's teaching. It isn't possible to believe that St Paul didn't know about these things. It's pretty certain that St Luke was writing his gospel in Rome at the same time when St Paul wrote some of his epistles; and they must have been seeing one another every day, but the two streams of Christian tradition didn't overflow into one another. Merely as a matter of literary curiosity, and quite apart from any bearing it has on religion, I should say that this lack of interdependence between the epistles and the gospels of the New Testament is a fascinating phenomenon, and in some ways a baffling one.

Of course, you might think it was open to anybody to suggest a perfectly simple solution. I mean, that St Paul didn't mention our Lord's miracles because he didn't believe in our Lord's miracles; that he didn't quote our Lord's teaching because it wasn't our Lord's teaching—the Evangelists were laboriously making it up out of their own heads at the very time when St Paul was writing. But obviously that doesn't do; because St Paul writes about Jesus of Nazareth as somebody only recently dead, whose actions were attested by a number of witnesses with whom he, St Paul, was familiar. Assuming that the account which the Evangelists give of our Lord's life is a faked account, why doesn't St Paul give us some of the *real* facts? Why doesn't he tell us who our Lord's father was, where our Lord was buried? But no, all the facts he does give us square out perfectly with what the gospels tell us. And the curious thing is, that they are just the things we might have found it difficult to believe. St Paul never mentions the fact that our Lord died except to lead up to the statement that he rose again from the dead. Nobody is more keen than St Paul to point out how our Lord came to deliver men from the bondage of the law, came to abolish the old Jewish ceremonies. Yet St Paul, in full agreement with the gospels, tells us how very strict our Lord himself was about the remarriage of divorced persons; tells us how our Lord instituted a ceremony which had to be observed as part of the very life of the Church. Our Lord, he says, was declared to be the Son of God, how? *Meta dunameos*, by miracle. There is nothing Broad Church, after all, about St Paul's writings.

You see how the person who is out to disprove the origins of Christianity is bothered all the time by this double stream of tradition, this double strand in the rope. On the one side St Paul, with his highly developed theology, not attempting to tell the story of how our Lord lived, hardly even alluding, just now and again in parenthesis, to some act or word of his; facts, you would say, bore him—he is only interested in ideas. On the other side, the Evangelists—I am thinking now of the first three Evangelists; St John evidently wrote a good deal later, and with different ideas in view—the first three Evangelists giving you their evidence utterly without comment, except to point out now and again the fulfillment of some Old Testament prophecy. They tell the most improbable stories without raising an eyebrow; they record the most extraordinary claims made by our Lord as if it were all the most natural thing in the world; they never improve the occasion, never take the reader by the button-hole and say, Now, look here, what do you really make of all this? No, they are simply historians, describing things as they appeared to the eyes of people who were there when they happened. Here is one curious little piece of literary restraint practised by St Matthew and St Mark. By the time they wrote, you can see it from St Paul's writings, it was common to refer to Jesus of Nazareth as "our Lord", or simply, "the Lord". St Luke does that a good many times; he obviously thought it the natural thing to do. But St Matthew and St Mark had such a fine instinct of telling the story as it happened, that the hero of it in their record is never referred to as "the Lord"; always they call him by his human name of Jesus. A plain, unvarnished narrative; they are content with the facts, ideas seem to frighten them.

However, I oughtn't to be talking to you about the Evangelists; that's somebody else's job. We ought rather to be considering the question, What is St Paul up to? Writing, as he did, when there were so many people going about who had witnessed the doings of the Incarnate, when the very accents of the Divine voice still echoed in Christian memory, why is he so economical in his references to the recent past, why, among all his innumerable quotations, does he quote so little from the teaching of his Master? Honestly I think the right key to it is a very obscure verse in that very obscure epistle, the second epistle to the Corinthians. "Christ died for us all," he says, "so that *being alive* should no longer mean living with our own life, but with his life who died for us and has risen again; and therefore, henceforward, we do not think of anybody in a merely human fashion; even if we used to think of Christ in a human fashion, we do so no longer." If he didn't dwell on the facts of our Lord's life, or even on the things our Lord said, it was, I suspect, because he didn't want his converts to think of our Lord as a piece of history, as the cherished memory of a dead person, as an individual man who lived at one particular moment in time. All that our Lord was; but for St Paul that was not the point. The point was that our Lord was alive; that he lived on in his body, his mystical body, the Church. When they met on the road to Damascus, our Lord said, "Why dost thou persecute *me*?", and that *me* remained in St Paul's thought as the keynote of all his theology.

No, they were not to think of Christ after a human fashion. His nature was Divine; if all things came *from* the Eternal Father, they came from him *through* Christ, and that *through* denoted, not a less ultimate responsibility, but somehow a more intimate relation. He was the Elder Brother of all created things, and it was suitable that when God determined to reconcile his rebel world to himself, Christ should be the focus in which all creation should be at once resumed and renewed. His nature was Divine, but the incommunicable privileges of Godhead were not allowed to detain him; somehow, he took upon himself the nature of Man, accepted all its inadequacies, shouldered all its responsibilities. He, our Elder Brother, our Representative, became our Victim, The Representative of our sin; hung upon the Cross, and, as if by the shock of that unparalleled encounter, shattered all the barriers that had existed till then—the barrier between God and Man, the barrier between life and death, the barrier between Jew and Gentile. He died, and in his death mankind, as mystically associated with him, died too, so that the old debt incurred by Adam's sin was cancelled. He rose again, and thereby acquired a second title to the headship of the human race; he was now the Elder Brother of all risen men. The life into which he rose was not a force that quickened his natural body merely; it quickened to birth a new, mystical Body of his, the Church. In the power of that life the individual Christian becomes supernaturally alive; dead to sin, dead to the fetters of the old legal observance, he lives now in Christ, lives now to God. Baptism, his initiation into his Master's death and resurrection, leaves him, as it were, gasping for breath and tongue-tied, while the Holy Spirit within him cries out "Father, Father", to claim the promise of adoption. Meanwhile, the Church as a whole is Christ's building, in which we all coinhere, is Christ's Bride, inspiring and prescribing sanctity, is Christ's Body, of which we are cells. Our whole life now is Christ-conditioned, he is the medium in which we exist, the air we breathe; all our nature is summed up, all our activities are given supernatural play, in him.

That is St Paul's programme; and perhaps it is not to be wondered at if he passes over in silence the details of a biography, whose total effect so reverberates with theological significance. The Incarnation, for St Paul, did not mean primarily that God had become *a* man; it meant primarily that God had become *Man*, had infected the human race, as it were, with his Divinity. "The Life of Christ" is a phrase which suggests to us, doesn't it, a book on a shelf, Père Didon or Archbishop Goodier or somebody like that. For St Paul, the phrase had no such meaning; or anyhow, that was not the meaning which immediately leaped to the mind. The Life of Christ was to him an energy that radiated all about him, was the very breath he drew in with his lungs. Do you know what it is to meet some great man, or even some interesting personality that arrests you, and to go away quite forgetting how he was dressed or even what he looked like, because the inspiration of what he said riveted you, so that you were unconscious of anything else? And even what he said hardly remains in the memory; what exactly *did* he say? You reflect, ruefully, that when you reach the age of eighty and sit down to write your reminiscences, the account given of this particular interview will look pretty silly. All you know is that a kind of glow pervades you, a kind of clarity seems to reveal your own thoughts to you, as the result of what passed. It is the man's personality that haunts you, something too subtle and elusive to admit of analysis, something beyond the play of features or the sound of speech; the man *himself* has cast a kind of spell on you. So it was with St Paul, I imagine, but in an infinitely higher degree, when he thought about Jesus of Nazareth; everything about him seemed irrelevant, seemed only secondary, compared with what Jesus of Nazareth was in himself.

I want you to see how providentially this attitude on the part of St Paul contrives to fill in, for our minds, the portrait of our Lord given to us by the first three Evangelists. After all, a portrait, however accurate and however revealing, doesn't really give you the man himself unless you knew the man himself. And I think there is, about the Synoptic gospels, a kind of deliberate objectiveness which sometimes makes it hard to understand the way in which their story develops. Why did the Apostles leave their nets and follow without a word, when our Lord said "Follow me"? What was the magic of voice or look that drew them away, in those early days when no miracles had yet been done, when the campaign of preaching had not yet been opened? Something escapes us in the narrative; what we call, in the loose sense, "personality". (I say in the loose sense, because philosophically speaking our Lord had no human personality; it was the one human thing he hadn't got.) The tremendous impact which his force of character made on people—do you remember how, according to St John, his captors in the garden went back and fell to the ground when he said, "I am Jesus of

Nazareth"?—all that is difficult to realize in the Synoptists. It becomes easier to realize when you watch the effect it had on St Paul; how, after that interview on the Damascus road, he saw Christ in everyone, Christ in everything, nothing but Christ.

One more suggestion I would add about St Paul's witness to the truth of the New Testament record. Except in one or two of his epistles, the Ephesians for example and the Colossians, he is not setting out to instruct his readers in the faith. He takes the faith for granted; he is arguing with his converts about their quarrels with one another, about their want of discipline, about the next collection he wants to take up, and so on; his are genuine letters, provoked by actual situations, not philosophical treatises disguised under a literary mask; we ought to call them letters, really, not "epistles". And that means that you have the man's honest convictions in front of you; he is not playing up to you at all, he is not laboriously working out a system of theology as he goes along. No, these dogmatic asides, these dogmatic overtones, overflow from the fullness of his heart. Within two decades of the Crucifixion, a whole elaborate theology of the Trinity and the Incarnation has already emerged as part of the fixed belief of Christians; you could appeal to it without any fear that your readers would suddenly jib and complain, "Here, what's all this?" Tell me, was he any ordinary Man, the Founder of Christianity, that the recent memory of his unassuming passage through the world should produce such repercussions as these?

11

Miracles

I have to speak about the evidence afforded by our Lord's miracles and in particular by his resurrection from the dead, in support of the claim that he was a fully accredited ambassador, bringing a unique revelation from God to man. The classical way of putting that argument is familiar to your memories, and would have suggested itself, in any case, to your common sense. The laws of nature are God's laws; *only* God can supersede them, by calling a higher, supernatural law into play. Or, putting it more scholastically, God ordinarily works through secondary causes, curing a disease, for example, by the use of some remedy. If we find a large number of people suddenly cured of their diseases without the use of any remedy at all, then the only possible conclusion is that God, who is the primary cause of all things, has seen fit here and here and here to dispense with secondary causes altogether. Why should he do that, always in connexion with the ministry of one Man, Jesus Christ, unless he wanted us to see that this Man was his favoured Servant? Now, this Man claimed that he had come to bring a unique revelation from God to the human race. Was he an impostor? If so, would God have bolstered up his false claim, his blasphemous claim, by enabling him to do miracles? Obviously not. Therefore, unless you can dispose of the miracles, you have got to admit that the claim made by Jesus of Nazareth was true.

That argument is met by the critics of the Christian religion in two different, in two quite incompatible ways. One is to say that miracles don't happen—we have never met one; and therefore miracles can't happen—if we thought they could, it would destroy all our confidence in the law of uniformity. The other way is to say that miracles are always happening, all the time; the Yogis do miracles, and the dervishes do miracles, and the Spiritualists do miracles, and the Christian Scientists do miracles. Either, then, what we call miracles are not really beyond the compass of human possibility, they depend on natural laws which we don't happen to have discovered yet—and in that case, there is no reason for believing that the message delivered by Jesus of Nazareth was true. Or else these other religions are being bolstered up by genuine miracles; and in that case the Yogi and the dervish and Daniel Home and Mary Baker Eddy must be regarded as teachers of true religion side by side with Jesus of Nazareth. Generally, if you get arguing about miracles with somebody who doesn't believe in religion, you will find that he starts the evening by saying that miracles are impossible, and ends it up by saying miracles are so common he really can't see why one should take any notice of them.

The answer to the first objection is an old and a comparatively simple one. We are not being rude to the uniformity of nature when we assert that miracles do sometimes happen. On the contrary, the exception proves the rule; it is because we believe in the uniformity of nature under ordinary conditions that miracles impress us, as proving to us that the conditions under which these events have happened must be extraordinary. Nobody is going to persuade us that miracles are impossible; because nothing can be called strictly impossible except what is inconceivable. And it is not inconceivable that when you let go of a book, say, it should fly up to the ceiling instead of dropping to the floor. Actually it doesn't, but that is because God happens to have arranged things that way; he might just as well have arranged them the other way. The law of gravitation isn't a self-evident thing, like the principle "Things that are equal to the same thing are

equal to one another." That is necessary by a necessity of
thought; God can't prevent them being equal to one other.
But the law of gravitation is, of its own nature, the sort of
law he might repeal overnight.

The other attitude, which says miracles are always happening all over the place, is much more difficult to deal with.
After all, we haven't the time to go all through all the stories
of miraculous occurrences in history, investigate all the psy-
chical phenomena of our own day, and prove them false
before we accept the evidence of the Christian miracles; life
is too short. The answer I want to indicate is this. We don't
assert the divineness of the Christian religion *merely* on the
strength of the miracles which our Lord is said to have per-
formed. We base our argument on the combined claim of his
miracles and his spiritual witness. The combined claim—
they aren't like two strands in a cable; they interpenetrate one
another, each supplements the other. And what we complain
about when we consider the phenomena of spiritualism, or
any of the more sensational stories that are quoted at us, is
that their setting, their background, is not really religious; it
has not the moral elevation about it which the Christian
miracles possess. It is just miracle for the sake of showing off;
and very frequently it degenerates into the idiotic. Sir William Crookes, the great scientist who went in for spiritualism,
told some friends of his the following story, which he swore
to. They had been doing some experiments in table-turning;
and after a bit they stopped using the particular table they had
been sitting at, and used another table, because it was more
convenient. And then, when nobody was touching either,
the table they had first used saw a chance of getting its own
back, and went for the other table, and there was a battle
royal between them. Now, the obvious comment, when you
get your breath back, is that the internecine feuds of drawing-
room furniture have no spiritual interest for us. All these odd
stories people tell, *if* they are true, must have some explanation which is of no importance for our views of eternity.

But the Christian miracles—I don't mean all the stories told about the saints, some of them are pretty odd, but the gospel miracles, anyhow—come to us wrapped up in a spiritual context which demands that they should have a spiritual interpretation. There is nothing of vulgar, thaumaturgic display about what our Lord did. Without effort, without preparation, without artificially prepared conditions, he imposed his will on nature, and always *in a religious context*.

I know there are lots of good people, Christian or half-Christian, who say they would rather not believe he did anything miraculous; it spoils their idea of him, and of God. They don't like to think of God breaking, so to put it, his own laws. Well, the simplest answer to them is that the thing can't be done. You can't purge the gospels of their miraculous element without discrediting the gospels altogether. If we believe that our Lord was ever born, we believe it on the same authority which tells us that his was a miraculous birth. If we believe that he ever died, we believe it on the same authority which tells us that he rose from the dead. Miracle haunts the story, at every turn. And—this is the one point I am trying to make now—miracle *suits* the story; it harmonizes with the situation which the gospels depict. To wish away the gospel miracles is not only to ask for something you can't get; it is to ask for something no reasonable person ought to want.

You see, if we're right, if the appearance of our Lord Jesus Christ among us was what it claimed to be, God's unique self-revelation made, once for all, to man—then it was fitting, you may say it was natural, if one can use such a word in such a connexion, that miracle should be its atmosphere. You couldn't, obviously, have spirituality at a higher level than the level at which our Lord taught it; you couldn't, obviously, have a man who lived his teaching more than our Lord did. And yet, neither his teaching nor his life, if you read them apart from the background of miracle, can be pronounced self-evidently divine. Simply because the human instruments he used, a human body, a human tongue, a human mind, a human soul, cannot produce natural results which, viewed in themselves, are more than human. If our Lord had come without doing any miracles, like St John the Baptist, he would have created a profound impression on his contemporaries, as St John the Baptist did; probably he would have left behind him a sect which might have lasted for centuries, a little group of choice souls who drew inspiration from the unforgotten record of his life. But this revelation he came to bring was to be a lever to shift the world with. And the mere pattern of a perfect human life wouldn't have done that. Our memories are too short, our loyalties too weak, our critical instincts too rebellious.

Our Lord's coming, if it was what we think it was, must be regarded as nothing less than an invasion of the natural by the supernatural world. And when it is confronted with the supernatural, the reaction of the natural world can only express itself in miracle. When Richard Crashaw, the poet, was asked to write a copy of Latin verses about the miracle at Cana of Galilee, he took the full time allotted to him, whatever it was, in writing a single pentameter. I have seen it quoted in different forms, but the form I like best is *Vidit et erubuit conscia lympha Deum*—the conscious water saw its Lord, and blushed. The conscious water, caught out in being what it was, just natural water, in the presence of something supernatural; it blushed, what else could it do? at the thought of its own inadequacy, its own perishableness; and the result was what we call a miracle. And yet, how natural that it should, given the supernatural!

Our minds are so limited, we always think of the supernatural world as something pale and imaginary and unsubstantial, compared with our own. But if you come to think of it, it's just the other way round. Ours is the world of shadows and of make-believe; the supernatural is real reality, with dimensions, so to speak, which ours does not guess at. When the sun shines in through the window onto the fireplace, it seems to put the fire out; some people have a super-stition that it does put the fire out. So it is, so it must be, surely, when the supernatural order breaks in upon the natu-ral. The lower order of being shrinks away, with unaccus-tomed reactions. If you think of our Lord walking on the water, your first instinct will be that of the Apostles, to imag-ine him a ghost, without substance and therefore without weight. Think, rather, of the water as coming in contact with the supernatural and losing, by virtue of that contact, the unsubstantial quality which makes it give under a man's weight. The light shines in darkness, and the darkness cannot catch up with it, cannot hold its own, but must needs give way, in a more or less degree, to the light's influence. All the deficiency, all the inadequacy of the natural world is dis-placed, somehow, by the contact of the supernatural. The diseases, the leprosy, the deafness, the blindness, the disfigured and distorted limbs, the paralysis—they are all part of the world's darkness; and when the light shines, the darkness yields to it; this positive thing overawes our negations; the sick get well, the blind see, and so on. It is miracle, yes, in the natural order; and yet if you think what the supernatural is, the wonder would be if these strange results didn't follow, when the supernatural breaks in upon us as it did at the Incarnation.

Think that out for yourself; I haven't time to develop it. I want to point out something else to you, that our Lord's teaching and his miracles are interlocked, because his miracles were teaching miracles. We know that from St John. If you read St John's account of how the five thousand were fed, you will find that the miraculous part only takes up the first twenty-one verses in a chapter which contains seventy-one verses. Those fifty verses at the end are all devoted to show-ing what the miracle means. Our Lord, no doubt, had all sorts of reasons for wanting to feed the five thousand; one was that they were hungry, which was a good reason in itself. But one reason was that he was deliberately preparing the ground for the Sacrament of the Holy Eucharist. You know how people after dinner, telling a story, will illustrate what happened by moving knives and salt-cellars and so on about, to illustrate how the land lay? Well, just so, our Lord in this miracle uses the common need of hunger, the common substance of bread, to give his hearers a sort of diagram of the supernatural life, and how it has needs, and how those needs are to be satisfied. So with the blind man who was sent to wash in the pool of Siloe; it was all a lesson in the meaning of baptism—the enlightenment from above which is necessary to all of us if we are going to open our eyes onto a spiritual world. And there are other miracles where we haven't been given the clue, but can see the lesson clearly enough for ourselves. The water turned to wine—our poor human effort transformed and energized by grace. The fig-tree that withered—God's judgement on the life that runs to leaf and bears no fruit. The swine at Gadara—how the madness of one man can drive a whole nation to its ruin. The palsied man, carried in by his friends and let down through the roof—how faith can triumph over obstacles, how prayer can avail for others besides ourselves. The miraculous draught of fishes—the blind obedience, the untiring patience which faith demands of us. The stilling of the tempest on the lake— what confidence we ought to derive from the presence of our Master in and with his Church. All working up to that astonishing miracle, the raising of Lazarus—the human soul, dead in sin, the prey of corruption, reawakened and disinterred.

And if you can say that of the miracles our Lord did in the course of his ministry, still more evidently is it true of those two great miracles which are the terminal landmarks of his human life; the Virgin Birth by which he came into the world, and the way of Resurrection by which he left it. At these terminal points, the invasion of the supernatural world shakes nature to its depths. Matter and Life, the two main conditions of our mortality, are challenged by this contact with a higher order of things. Matter must see its own laws defied, when a Man comes into the world leaving his Mother still a Virgin, when he goes out of the world leaving the stone and the seal of his virgin tomb unviolated. Life must see its own laws defied, when he comes into the world unbegotten, when he goes out of the world alive. And, as before, these wonders are not sent to dazzle us, they are sent to enlighten us. We see, in the Virgin Birth, the promise of our own regeneration by the Holy Spirit in the womb of the Church. We see, in the Resurrection, the sowing of that seed of immortality which is to take root in us too, quicken us with new life and make us, too, immortal.

Don't think that I am trying to allegorize away these Christian miracles we are speaking of. On the contrary, my point is that they have *at once* historical fact and theological meaning. Take the Resurrection as an instance; the crucial item in the whole list. It is documented history; you can read how our Lord challenged his persecutors with the promise that he would raise the temple of his own body from death; how they, when they had secured his death, secured, too, the place of his burial with every detail of precaution. How the body disappeared, when nobody had any interest in its disappearance except a handful of panic-stricken fugitives; when it was in the soldiers' interest to carry out their commission, when it was in Pilate's interest to safeguard the tomb, against the possibility of further rioting, when it was in the Jews' interest to be able to say, No, he has not risen, here is his body. How the Man who had died on his Cross was seen again, not by people who were expecting his return, and ready to identify any chance stranger with the person they were looking for, but by people who did not expect his return, and, meeting him, took him at first to be a chance stranger—Mary Magdalen in the garden, the disciples on the road to Emmaus, the ten Apostles in the Upper Room, the seven Apostles by the lake of Galilee. He points to the scars left by his Passion; he eats and drinks with them. A few weeks later, the disappearance of the body is a fact which you can refer to before a public audience as a fact which everybody recognizes. If that is not history, how shall history ever be written?

And yet, if you read St Paul's epistles, written such a short time afterwards—the earliest of them only a matter of twenty years afterward—you will find the historical fact of the Resurrection almost swallowed up in the doctrinal significance of the Resurrection. Oh, St Paul does appeal to the fact of the Resurrection as a ground for belief in the Christian religion; he is quite orthodox, is St Paul. But much oftener, much more characteristically, his thought passes straight from the Resurrection to the meaning of the Resurrection in our lives. "You have been baptized, haven't you? Very well then, in baptism you were buried with Christ, buried in Christ's tomb. Buried there, buried in such company, you have, necessarily, risen again. You are living, therefore, with a new life; your old, worldly existence lies behind you, a dead past. Very well, then, no more sin for you. No more quarreling for you, no more backbiting for you, no more incontinence for you. You have risen, and your life is hidden with Christ in God."

You see, then, what I've been trying to say, so inadequately, in so short a time. We mustn't let people think of our Lord's miracles as if they were a set of theatrical performances, thrown out by a well-known preacher in order to draw attention to himself. They are part of his message; a sign-language between heaven and earth, pictures of eternity cast onto the screen of time. It's convenient for us, as a matter of arrangement, to have a conference one Sunday about the witness of our Lord's life and teaching, and on another Sunday a conference about the witness of our Lord's miracles. But in fact they are woof and warp of the same fabric. Say, if you will, that his miracles come to us bathed in the light of his teaching. Or say, if you will, that his teaching comes to us pegged down to reality—supernatural reality—by his miracles. But you must examine his life as a whole, as a unity, not broken up into strands, if you are really to understand the part which it plays in establishing the truth, and the divine origin, of that Church which he founded, and of that teaching which he entrusted to her.

12

The Claim of Christ

I suppose there has been no subtler attack upon the Christian faith devised by its enemies in these last hundred years than the attack made in the name of "comparative religion". If you pick up a book on "Atonement", and plough your way through ideas of atonement among primitive tribes, pagan ideas of atonement, Jewish ideas of atonement, Christian ideas of atonement, you will find that by the end of it atonement, for the author's mind, has ceased to have any meaning. And he has been successful, in so far as he has managed to infect your mind with the woolliness which is the leading characteristic of his own. Comparative religion is an admirable recipe for making people comparatively religious.

And the same kind of pitfall awaits us, when we have reached that point in apologetics which we are supposed to have reached now. Let us remind ourselves where we stand. You were considering the arguments for the existence of God, and the notions about his Divine attributes which can be legitimately derived from natural theology. Then, you went on to revelation. You found, in the Old Testament, the way made ready, the train laid, as it were, for the invasion of our world by the supernatural. You saw something of what it was that our Lord claimed to be, and of the arguments which can be adduced to show that his claim is valid. And then, just when you think you've got all that taped, if you try to work it off on an unbelieving friend, you will find that he has still got a shot left in his locker. "That's all very well," he will say,

"I quite see that you Christians have more arguments in support of your view than I ever thought possible. But, if I were to adopt a religion, I shouldn't be content to take Christianity just because you happen to have thrown it at me, like a shopkeeper who says I must have this kind of electric torch because it is the only one he's got left. I should want to take a good look-round, as we did in the days of old-fashioned, peace-time shopping, and see whether there wasn't, perhaps, some other religion in the world which had claims more convincing than yours, which had an atmosphere which suited me even better than yours. Till I had done that, I shouldn't think it honest to call myself a Christian. And I really haven't got time to go into all that."

Well, you can see the surface plausibility of the suggestion; how are we to counter it in the space of half an hour? I thought what we would do would be this: let's consider whether there isn't a secret fallacy about this idea that you can compare Christianity with other religions as if they were all on the same level; as if religion meant being a Confucian or a Muslim or a Buddhist or a Christian or *something of that sort*. I think there is a fallacy, and it's really the fallacy of many questions. When you compare Christianity with Confucianism, you are comparing two systems of personal morality. When you compare Christianity with Mahomedanism, you are comparing two forms of fighting enthusiasm. When you compare Christianity with Buddhism, you are comparing two streams of mystical tendency. And, unconsciously, you have recognized that Christianity is something greater than the other three; because each of those others corresponds to one particular need, one particular mood, of man, whereas Christianity corresponds to all three.

Let me expand that a little. There are some natures, there are some moods of our nature, for which religion means moral inspiration. The burden of daily living weighs so heavily, it is so dull being good, so irksome being kind, it is so hard to put up with our disappointments and our discomforts, that we want to get hold of some good book or even go and listen to a sermon, to brace up our moral tone a bit. A man of such a nature, a man in such a mood, can easily be imagined as halting before his book-case and asking, Shall it be Confucius, or Christ? To other people, religion is primarily a matter of culture; to defend your own culture against attack, to enhance its influence, even to propagate it by means of coercion, is the great business of life. And it is not unnatural, perhaps, for the historian who is studying the Middle Ages, to feel a kind of professional doubt about the Crusades. Was the heroism, he asks himself, all on the side of the Christians? Were the atrocities all on the side of the Turk? And would it, perhaps, have made no great difference if the Christians had conquered Mecca, or if the Mussulmans had conquered Rome, when there were the same virtues, the same weaknesses, on both sides? Again, there are those minds, of rarer spiritual temper, to which religion means an escape above and beyond the empty shows of sense, the unification of all our experience in some higher experience which is neither sensation nor thought, a repose of all our faculties in the contemplation of the Unseen. Such a mind may plausibly argue, Well, here is the mysticism of Buddha, here is the mysticism of St John of the Cross; is there really so much difference between them? At these levels of spiritual experience, do we not shed our theologies like unnecessary clothes, and penetrate to the common heart of all religion? Why should I label myself Christian, or Buddhist, when it all comes to the same thing?

You see what I mean? When you compare the message of Christ with that of some other world-teacher, you are always isolating one aspect of it, and forgetting the rest. I have given you three instances, but you could find any amount more. You may compare Christianity with Spiritualism as a philosophy of life and death; you may compare Christianity with Christian Science as an attitude towards health and disease; you may compare Christianity with Communism as a formula for attacking economic problems. But always, in doing so, you are thinking of Christianity only under one aspect. You are like a mathematician who should gravely contrast the size of a sphere with that of a series of circles. Let us stick to the three comparisons we started with, for the sake of clearness.

The Sermon on the Mount is an incomparable document, as a guide to human conduct. If you read it through in some edition with notes, which gives you the quotations from the Old Testament included in it, and the sayings of the Rabbis which seem, now and then, to echo its teaching, you will be all the more struck by its divine originality. But we should never, in argument, allow ourselves to be manoeuvred into the position which implies, as so many modern teachers imply, that the Sermon on the Mount *is* Christianity. More than a dozen years ago, when I was writing a book about the journalist's idea of religion, I was at pains to copy out the Teaching of Christ, in the sense in which journalists will talk to you about "the Teaching of Christ". Do you know how much space it occupied? Two printed pages and a little bit over. Two printed pages and a little bit over, extracted from the whole of St Matthew's Gospel, which occupies about ninety pages of print! All about loving our enemies, and not judging one another, and the tree being known by its fruits. Well, I dare say you could dig out a good deal of that from poor old Confucius. But that is only a tiny fraction of what Christ's teaching really was. He taught the world about its need of redemption, about its need of revelation, and showed it that both were to be found, in himself. He taught the world that the Old Covenant which God made with the Jews was being abolished, and that he was once more choosing out for himself a people of his own—only this time it was not to be one nation, it was to be a world-wide assembly of ransomed souls. He offered the world a religion, not a code of ethics.

It would be very easy to spend our time comparing

Christianity with Confucianism as a system of morals. As far
as I understand it, Confucianism depends largely on worshipping your ancestors; hardly a suitable doctrine for our modern Western world, in which we spend so much of our time
pointing out that our ancestors were barbarians, and fools at
that. But the important thing is that Christianity is not just a
system of morals; that is only one side of it. Our Lord didn't
come to give us a set of helpful quotations to print in calen-
dars. He came to tell us about himself. Did Confucius ever
say, "All power is given to me in heaven and in earth"? Did
Mahomet ever say, "No one cometh to the Father but by
me"? Did Buddha ever say, "Whoever confesseth me before
men, the same will I confess before my Father who is in
heaven"? And that was the teaching of Christ.

The people who think of Christianity in that way are
commonly the well-meaning people who regard themselves
as its friends. Its enemies—and it has plenty of enemies nowadays—look upon Christianity rather as a special kind of
culture, like the Mahomedan. Indeed, very like the Mahomedan. Both these two cultures started in the East, both had
the instinct of world-conquest, both regarded loyalty to your
own particular set of religious catch-words as the highest
form of virtue, capable of bringing you a rich reward in a
future life. If you lived south of the Mediterranean, you
believed in one God, and Mahomet as his prophet; if you
lived north of the Mediterranean, you believed in one God,
and Jesus of Nazareth as his prophet. In the one case, you
held strict views about wine, in the other case you held strict
views about women. In the Middle Ages, the two cultures
came into violent conflict, and for some centuries it looked
as if one or the other must go under, probably the Christian.
In the end, Europe remained mostly Christian, Western Asia
and Northern Africa mostly Mahomedan. Both are anti-
quated, unsuited to modern conditions, and therefore likely
to disappear. It is in those terms, I say, that the enemies of
Christianity think of us. And anybody whose mind is in-

fected with that sort of language might plausibly ask, Why do you want me to become a Christian? Why not a Mahomedan, while I'm about it? You must surely give me grounds for making up my mind between the two.

The same mistake, you see, made this time from a different angle. There is such a thing as Christian culture, but it is not the same thing as Christianity. Once more we might, if we pleased, devote some of our time to comparing the two, as cultures, and giving reasons for preferring our own; Mahomedan views about women, Mahomedan views about slavery, are not (or used not to be) such as would commend themselves to the prejudices of Western Europe. But once again I think the important point to make is, that whether or not Christianity is a better type of culture than Islam, Christianity is something more than a type of culture, and Islam, when you come to look into it, is not. Islam spread by military conquest; its fortunes were the fortunes of a particular race. You rallied to it as a kind of old school tie; you did not ask yourself whether the history recorded in the Koran was true history or not. And of course it is possible to regard the Crusades as a kind of vast Eton-and-Harrow, in which both sides rallied to their respective ties by instinct, rather than by reasoned preference. While the Christian shouted *"Dieu le veult"*, the Mahomedan shouted "Great is Allah!"; what was, to the Christian, a crusade, was to the Mahomedan, a Jehad, a holy war; while the Christian hoped to get indulgences by it, the Mahomedan was assured that if he were killed fighting in such a cause, his soul would go straight to heaven. Look upon it as a struggle between two rival cultures, and you will not, perhaps, find much reason (apart from inherited prejudice) for backing one side rather than the other. But Christianity was something more than a culture; it was a philosophy, and Mahomedanism was not really a philosophy. You can prove that by a rather curious test.

Just at the same time when the Crusades were being fought,

another battle was being fought in the world of ideas. Aristotle was rediscovered, and the rediscovery produced a great fluttering both in Christian and Mahomedan dovecotes. Because hitherto Plato had had it all his own way, and Plato seemed obviously a respectable sort of philosopher for religious people to believe in. The come-back of Aristotle was at first opposed by the theologians, whether of Christendom or of Islam; and the effect of his influence on many minds was to set them all wrong about the first principles of theism. But whereas, among the Mahomedans, the thing remained a battle between the philosophers and the theologians and the theologians won, in the Christian Church (though not without difficulty) a synthesis was effected between the new philosophy and the old orthodoxy. That is the achievement of St Thomas. We took over Aristotle, and made a Christian of him. Oh, the Arabs were excellent mathematicians, excellent doctors—much better doctors than the Christians. But when it came to pure philosophy, we could assimilate the new ideas, and they couldn't. We digested Aristotle; they swallowed him and then—well let's say they coughed him up. That's why I say that Mahomedanism was a good fighting religion, but not really a good thinking religion. Put the Christian and the Moslem opposite one another in battle, and there is not much to choose. Make philosophy the test, and you see the difference.

And, you know—although this is a fact people don't often call attention to—our Lord did mean his religion to be a religion which could be argued. He argued himself, and argued very effectively. It's true that, since he was a Jew talking to Jews, he assumed for the purposes of argument what was common ground between him and them—the truth of the Old Testament prophecies. But look how he calls them in evidence; "If David then called Christ his Lord, how can Christ be his son?"—the whole theology of the Incarnation was in that challenge, and of course the Pharisees couldn't answer it. But it wasn't only when he was putting down his opponents that he had recourse to the argument from prophecy. He expected his own followers to be able to use it, and to recognize him, consequently, as the Christ. "O fools, and slow of heart to believe", "Thus it was written, thus it behoved Christ to suffer"—he actually reproaches them for having been disheartened over his death, because if they had taken the trouble to work out the implications of the old prophecies, they would have seen that death and resurrection were a necessary episode in the Christ's career. Our Lord thanked God for having concealed his mysteries from the wise and prudent, and revealed them to babes. But he didn't expect our faith to be a blind act of faith; it was to have a reasoned basis behind it. He came to preach the Truth, not merely to arouse a prejudice.

But God forbid that we should think of the Christian religion merely as a philosophy, or even merely as a theology. I say again, it is a sphere, not a disc. And for the most part, our Lord's closest friends have not been learned people who knew how to argue in favour of his religion, but simple people who have known how to live it. Not to know about God, but to know God—that is the ambition of the mystic. And, as I say, when you reach the higher levels of mystical experience, the same trouble crops up—we are asked how Christianity differs, so far as mystical experience is concerned, from other religions, and in so far as it does, whether it differs for the better. Those of you who read Mr Aldous Huxley's *Grey Eminence*, if that book is not already forgotten, will remember that he wants us to look on the best Christian mysticism as hardly distinguishable, if it is distinguishable at all, from the mysticism of the East. People like St John of the Cross—he does not make quite so free with St Teresa— would really, he insinuates, have felt quite at home in Bud- dhism. And once more you are up against the same objection, though this time a slightly different twist has been given to it, "Why should I be a Christian? Why not a Buddhist, while I'm about it?"

Well, I think there is a good deal that could be said about
the differences which distinguish Christian mysticism from
other mysticisms, in spite of external resemblances. As for
instance, that the kind of mysticism which Mr Huxley goes
in for seems to start entirely from the human end. You want
to get away from the distractions of earth, forget about the
war, for instance, and retreat into yourself and become one
with the eternal Thought, and so on. But Christian mysticism starts from God's end; it is only because he is so bowled
over by the consciousness of God that the Christian mystic
wants to do anything about it at all. But, once again, the
point for us is not to prove that Christianity is better than
Buddhism viewed as a form of mysticism. It is enough for us
to reiterate that Christianity is something else besides mysticism, whereas Buddhism is precious little else. You must not
be content to compare the Buddhist saint with the Christian
saint; you must compare the Buddhist sinner with the Christian sinner. The religion of Christ is not only for those
favored souls who can manage to leave this earth on the
wings of contemplation. It is for struggling souls too, all
blinded by the blood and sweat of the world's conflict, half
caught in the mire of its beastliness, and yet somehow keeping hold of that Christ who pardoned the adulteress, and
saved his doubting apostle from being swallowed up by the
waves.

Our Lord's claim is not just to satisfy this or that need of
common life, meet this or that situation in common life. He
offers to give us a new, supernatural life, complete with all its
faculties, in the midst of this troubled and precarious world.
No one else offers us that; no one else dares claim of us the
faith which will enable us to believe in that. Reject him if
you will, but do not try to match him with the world's other
teachers. He will not be content to take his place in a series;
he is nothing, if he is not unique.

13

The Four Marks of the Church

When we have come to the conclusion that our Lord founded a Church, we have still to ask a further question, Which Church? That need not surprise or scandalize us; it's the good things in the world, not the bad things, that produce a crop of imitations—people imitate Keats, they don't imitate Ella Wheeler Wilcox.

This good wine that Christ has given us—it is only natural, in an imperfect world, that there should be some confusion about the labels. In order to keep our heads, when we start out to look for the true Church, we remember that in the *Credo* at Mass it is qualified by four distinguishing marks, "I believe in one, holy, Catholic, and Apostolic Church." Those four marks must be present in the body we are looking for. And this is worth observing; we must be content if we find that they are there at all, we must not expect, necessarily, to find them in an eminent degree. That is a common experience when you are dealing with definitions. The usual definition of Man is that he is a reasoning animal; he is *Homo Sapiens*. And that is true, you see, even of lunatics; they reason, in fact they often reason with great acuteness, like the mad don who thought the don underneath was trying to shoot him through the floor, and consequently always sat on the table until at last he grew to believe that he was a tea-pot. At the same time, when you reflect on this definition of man, and realize that sapience is his characteristic quality, it makes you examine your conscience a bit, and wonder whether, having matriculated at a University, you ought not to be trying to become a little more sapient. And so it is, as I shall try to point out, with these four marks of the Church. They show us what it is, and at the same time they encourage us, in our small way, to try and make it rather more so.

To prove that the Church is, and is meant to be, visibly one, is pretty easy going. You've only to read St Paul's epistles to be struck by the enormous importance which he attaches to the unity of the Church. It's quite true that he will talk about the church at Corinth, say, and the church at Thessalonica, but never with the smallest suggestion that they are two separate entities. No, it's just like talking about the air at Brighton and the air at Blackpool; the Church, for St Paul, is the atmosphere in which a Christian moves and has his being; even when some half-dozen slaves in some rich person's household had been converted to Christianity, St Paul used to speak of the Church in So-and-so's household. And heavens, how he is always going on and on at those early Christians, even then, about unity; telling them to be built up into one another, to grow up into a single body, and so on. For St Paul, the Church is at once something wholly united, and something wholly unique. The Bride of Christ, how could there be more than one Bride of Christ? The building of which Christ is the cornerstone; what more compact idea could you get of Christian fellowship? The Body of which Christ is the Head; how could there be more than one such Body, or how, outside the unity of that Body, can a man have a right to think of himself as united to Christ?

Of course, you may object that St Paul perhaps wasn't thinking of what *we* mean by the Church; he was thinking of the invisible Church, as it has sometimes been called—not a society of people distinguishable here and now by possessing a common faith and a common organization, but simply an ideal concept, the sum total of those souls whose names will, at last, be found written in the book of life. Only, you see, that won't do, because our Lord himself doesn't think of the Church in that way. The kingdom of heaven (which was his name for it) is like a mixed crop, part of it wheat, part of it cockle, only to be separated at the final judgement; it is like a net cast into the sea, which brings up fish for the dinner-table and fish which are of no use to anybody, not to be separated till the net is brought in to land. The Church, then, as Christ himself envisaged it is a visible Church, rogues and honest men mixed; not all members of the Church are bound for heaven by any means.

And if you look round, today, for a visible Church which is visibly one, there is hardly any competition, is there? I mean, Christians who belong to other denominations don't even claim, as a rule, that their denomination is *the* Church. Church unity is something which existed in the early ages, which will, it is to be hoped, come into existence again later on; it doesn't exist here and now. Anybody who has reached the point of looking round to find a single, visible fellowship of human beings which claims to be the one Church of Christ, has got to become a Catholic or give up his search in despair.

At the same time, if you get arguing with non-Catholics about the unity of the Church, you will find they have a complaint to make about it. Isn't yours (they ask) rather a nominal kind of unity? Why did the German Catholics allow Hitler to invade Catholic Poland? Why do the Catholic Italians persecute the Catholic Jugo-Slavs? And so on—you know the kind of thing. Well, here we have to go back to the principle I was laying down just now; we said unity, not perfect unity. There have been times at which Pope and Antipope reigned side by side, dividing the sympathies of Europe. But even then, there was only one Church. Part of Christendom followed the true Pope; part of it in good faith, materially but not formally in schism, followed the Antipope. A man suffering from schizophrenia is still *homo sapiens*. A Church united in doctrine and in ecclesiastical theory is still one Church, although its energies are being dissipated in schism.

Meanwhile—this is the other side of the picture—we Catholics ought to be a jolly sight more careful than we are about unity. It's quite true we have got a central executive in Rome which can, at a pinch, dispose of any controversy; but that is such an awfully bad reason for spending our whole time running controversies among ourselves, nation against nation, one religious order against another, one set or clique of lay people against another, the whole time. I've never yet been able to understand what it is that leads Catholics to savage one another so fiercely, the moment there is any difference of opinion. That is something we can do something about.

But I mustn't go on about that; we must consider the second mark, the holiness of the Church. Here we are in a somewhat more embarrassing position when we start arguing with our friends outside the Church; they're so apt to expect rather too much, aren't they? The usual explanation the books give of this second mark is that "holiness" in the Church is proved partly by the continuance of miracles within her fold, and partly by the existence of the religious orders, with their special cult of perfection. The Church (we are told) has her ups and downs, her bad patches here and there, but we've still got Lourdes and we've still got Carmel. I've no quarrel with that explanation, but I think you can put the thing rather more simply in this way—Christians of any other denomination, if they describe that denomination as "holy" at all (which they very seldom do), are referring in fact to the individual holiness of its members. Whereas when we talk about the Holy Catholic Church we aren't thinking, precisely, of the holiness of its members. We think of the Church as sanctifying its members, rather than being sanctified by its members. Sanctity—what a hard thing it is to define! There is a kind of *bouquet* of mystery about Catholic ceremonial, there is a kind of familiarity about the attitude of

Catholics towards death and what lies beyond death, there is a patient acceptance of little oddnesses and inconveniences about the practice of religion, which you don't find outside the Church itself, except perhaps among certain High Church people who have been at pains to imitate what is to us a natural attitude. That's all very vague, and I haven't time to analyze it more particularly; but I think the reason why atheists usually say, "If I was anything, I'd be a Catholic", is that there is a *something* about her; and that something is really her sanctity, a quality which belongs to the institution as such, not to you and me.

And that something is not affected, really, by all the mud-slinging which starts, among the more embittered kind of Protestants, the moment the sanctity of the Church is mentioned. Immoral popes and worldly bishops, and priests in odd parts of the world who aren't any better than they should be, and the massacre of St Bartholomew and a dozen other incidents which recall to us the dictum "Happy is the nation which has no history"—well, yes. All that we can admit, and regret, and refuse to extenuate, and still say, "Yes, I know, but I'd sooner be a Catholic than anything else, because I'm not much of a chap really, and somehow being a Catholic means feeling that you get something out of it, whereas being any other kind of Christian means feeling that you've got to put something into it." All that's true, and it's fine. But, mark you, the real reason why Catholic propaganda doesn't go down better than it does, is our individual unholiness. I don't so much mean the way Catholics are always appearing in the police-courts and so on; there's a lot to be said about that, and it's not all to our discredit. No, I mean rather our terrible second-rateness, our determination to get to heaven as cheaply as possible, the mechanical way in which we accept our religious duties, our habit of thinking about every problem of conduct in terms of sin and of hell, when we ought to be thinking much more about generosity in our treatment of God. "Nor knowest thou what argument thy life to thy neighbour's creed hath lent"—it isn't logic, but that's the real mark of the Church the world is looking out for, all the time.

And then, the Catholicity of the Church—there we feel on surer ground again. It's so obvious, on the one hand, that our Lord meant his Church to be an assembly of all the nations, in contradistinction to the old church of the Jews, which was simply the assembly of one nation; it doesn't need proving. And it's so obvious, on the other hand, that the Church which is in communion with Rome is a world-wide Church, does transcend merely local prejudices and merely local ways of thinking; that to be a Catholic does obliterate, instead of emphasizing, the sense of strangeness which you and I have when we meet a foreigner. Say what you will, the other Christianities are so hall-marked with their place of origin, reflect so perfectly a German, or an English, or an American outlook; even their virtues are so much the characteristic virtues of a particular and rather modern culture, that you can't think of their missionary influence, splendid as it often is, as a Catholicizing influence. Whatever else they dislike about us, men admire, and envy, our international ubiquity.

But don't let's forget that our critics have something to say on the other side. They complain that our Catholic culture, though on the face of it it is world-wide, is dominated by the influence of a particular group of nations. In the Middle Ages, Catholicism was at least pan-European. But now, if you lump together the Latin races, with Ireland and Poland, you can say roughly that these dominate Catholic culture; everywhere else the Church is represented by minorities. And there is a temper, they tell us, about Catholics which is just the opposite, somehow, of what we mean by the word Catholic. There's a jealous, a rather timorous attitude about Catholics which makes them look with suspicion on all ideas which haven't sprung from their own minds; there's a rather offensive tone of "Here's tae us, and wha's like us?" about a good deal of their literature; they're all, somehow, rather *shut in*. If the Church is Catholic in her geographical extension, is she really Catholic in the field of ideas?

Well, you'd want at least a whole conference to deal properly with that charge. There can be a lot of danger in the infiltration of ideas—the very word infiltration gives you, nowadays, the picture of sinister little men creeping through a jungle. I always remember the last of Dr Caird's famous lay sermons when I was at Balliol, and the terrific impressiveness, only possible to a Scot, with which he enunciated the words, "Remember, the man who shuts himself in shuts others out." I thought at the time, and still think, that that was a sort of parody of the Oxford Hegelian manner. Because, after all, what on earth do you *mean* by shutting yourself in, except that you are shutting other people out? But let us take his point, and let us admit for the sake of argument, at any rate, that the circle of the Church's ideas has been rather narrow, that its culture has been too much a specifically Latin culture, ever since the Reformation. That, if it is true, is not altogether our fault; ever since the Reformation, as Ward used to say, we have been in a state of siege; we have lived under a kind of martial law. If the Northern-European point of view is not sufficiently represented in the Church's councils, that is because the nations of Northern Europe, four hundred years ago, cut themselves off from the Church. It may be that as time goes on our Catholic culture—I do not say our Catholic faith, I only say our Catholic culture—will be further enriched by absorbing the thought of other nations; not necessarily European nations; we may have something to learn from Asia as well. But the point about the Church is that she has the power to assimilate, to digest, fresh ideas, instead of merely gulping them down; all her history makes us sure of that. And in that power of assimilation, she is Catholic.

Have we, as individual Catholics, a lesson to learn, here too? I hesitate to draw the moral, because as I say there are two sides to this question. And it may be urged that in England,

and especially in Oxford, we Catholics are in danger of ex-
changing our ideas too much with the outside world, rather
than too little. Let me only say this, for the benefit of anybody
here who may need the warning; don't fall into the tempta-
tion of crabbing everything that's not Catholic.

Catholic and Apostolic—that is a kind of concealed paradox. This Church which is to be a world-Church, must
therefore, you would think, have a breadth of outlook which
enables it to enter into the mind of each nation, and interpret
it to itself, is nevertheless Apostolic; it is committed to the
doctrine handed down, centuries ago, by a set of working
men in an obscure province of the Roman Empire. The
notion of apostolicity is the faithful handing on of a message.
Apostello, to send out, that is a key word of the New Testament; it occurs about 130 times in the course of it, quite
apart from the frequent use of the word "apostle". As the
Father hath sent me, even so I send you—that is the start of
the whole thing. In the Old Testament, you find the prophets
coming forward in obedience to an inward vocation from
God. In the New Testament, it is not enough to be called;
you must be sent; St Paul himself, a called man if ever there
was one, was sent by the Church at Antioch when he began
his travels. And that sending has been going on continuously
through the ages; the Church has always had her own hierarchy of commissioned officials, following one another in unbroken succession. The other denominations may claim that
their ministers are called; but who sent them? Always, if you
examine their line of succession, there is a flaw in the title-
deeds; a human agent has stepped in and interrupted, by his
interference, the unbroken succession of *sent men* to whom
our Lord made his promises.

Have our critics found a come-back, here too? Do they
accuse us of not being apostolic enough? Well, they haven't
the courage to say that we don't try to impress other people
with our ideas; if anything, their complaint is rather the
opposite. But they have managed to put us in our place, by

slightly altering the meaning of the word "apostolic". A funny thing (they say) that you should boast of direct descent from a set of Galilean peasants, when you have your sailing orders given you by a man dressed in very expensive clothes, who talks to you down a golden telephone from one of the few really magnificent palaces left in the world. What bank balances your religious houses have! Is that apostolic? How consistently clerical influence in politics tells in favor of the right, rather than the left; is that apostolic? Well, as I say, they have taken a certain amount of liberty with the word. The word they really want is not so much apostolic as apostoloid. But we mustn't quarrel with them over niceties of language. I don't think we need waste much time in discussing clerical incomes. In some parts of the world, it may be the clergy do themselves too well; in others, they are miserably poor. In England, I think we strike a fair mean; we don't live too well, considering that we are bachelors. There is more substance, I should say, in the accusation that a clerical party in politics is usually a party of the right. There is a terrible lot to be said about that on both sides, and I have allowed myself exactly no time for dealing with it. Let me only say this; that it is a good rule in life not to show the weaknesses which people expect you to show—it makes them take more notice. We are suspected, we Catholics, of having too little sympathy for the poor, for the under-dog. It is important, I think, for Catholics, whatever their views, not to justify that impression, sometimes by living too luxuriously, sometimes by thinking too explosively.

One, holy, Catholic, and Apostolic; those have always been the marks of the true Church; always will be, whatever we do or don't do about it. But, if you and I are to be true samples by which the quality of our Church can be judged, we have to be lovers of unity, generous in our dealings with God, generous in our attitude towards men who do not agree with us, and, in such measure as circumstances and opportunities allow, apostoloid.

14

Salvation outside the Church

It is one of the drawbacks of advancing years, that you never feel quite sure to what extent the coming generation has abandoned the idols of your youth. I mean, in literature and the arts and so on. There is one really important English author, as I see him—or rather, he was a Scot—who has fallen out of fashion a good deal and is now very commonly regarded as the sort of man who could tell a good yarn to boys, nothing much else; Robert Louis Stevenson. But Stevenson was something very much more than that; something very much more than a writer of melodious English prose. He and W. H. Mallock represent that mood of despair which fell upon the last age of Victorianism, when it looked as if religion had been shown up, and couldn't very well survive. Was it possible, they asked, to take an optimistic view of the universe, to believe that good is somehow the right explanation of it? Mallock wrote *Is Life Worth Living?* and years later received the last rites of the Church, when he was already unconscious, because he had obviously been making up his mind to become a Catholic. Stevenson died young, not in any recognizable sense a Christian, but after fighting, all his life, against that ultimate doubt which haunted him.

You get his attitude towards religion best implied—it is hardly stated—in those fables of his which are usually printed at the end of *Dr Jekyll and Mr Hyde*. I am only citing from memory what is, I think, the most depressing of them, the one called "The Yellow Paint". A quack doctor comes to a town and publishes an advertisement of his marvellous yellow paint; anybody who is coated with this is insured, roughly speaking, against all inconveniences in this world and the next. A young man comes in and gets himself done; as he walks away he is run over by a cab, and sends from hospital to ask the quack doctor why he has got a broken leg. Assured that, although he hasn't responded to treatment very well so far, he will be all right in the next world, he sends for the quack doctor again, and asks, "How is this? Gangrene has set in, and I am dying; and what is worse than that is that in spite of what you told me I am terribly frightened of death, and what lies beyond it. Where does your paint come in now?" And the doctor can only say, "Perhaps if you hadn't had the treatment you would be more frightened still."

Et secuti sumus te; quid ergo erit nobis—"We have forsaken all and followed thee, what shall we have therefore?" Inevitably the man who accepts the obligations of religion, even if it is only in a rather casual way, tends to think of it as a bilateral compact, a covenant. If this God is to be your God, he must, in return, regard you as his people. The Jews under the Old Dispensation mostly thought of this covenant as an undertaking on the part of God to make them happy and successful on earth; and a very large share of the Old Testament is devoted to examining the question why that expectation hasn't worked out according to schedule. Curiously, it was the heathen, in their mystery religions, who found it much easier to think of the rewards due to the worshipper as something which you must expect in an after-life, not in this life. Our Lord's attitude can be defined by his answer to the question St Peter asked, the one I have just quoted, "What shall we have therefore?" He replied unmistakably that his followers should be compensated for the sacrifices they made a hundredfold in this life, and that in the world to come they should have life everlasting.

With the rewards Christians get in this life, we are not

concerned at present; we must leave that on one side. Meanwhile, he has pledged himself to give us everlasting life in the world to come. If St Peter had approached his religion in that bargaining spirit of which we are sometimes guilty, he might have urged a supplementary question: "Will anybody else get everlasting life in the world to come? Or is it strictly reserved for those who forsake all things and follow you?" Suppose we put that question to ourselves, and try to infer the answer to it from the rest of our Lord's teaching. Always, he represents it as a matter of urgency to become a genuine citizen of his kingdom before the moment of judgement overtakes you, and it is too late. Outside, there will be weeping and gnashing of teeth. Not the undying worm, not the unquenchable fire; that destiny is only mentioned in connexion with people who refuse to get rid of hindrances to holiness. If you had only these scattered remarks of our Lord's to go upon, you might be inclined to imagine that there was a hell for obstinate sinners, and a kind of limbo for the people who simply missed their chances, through indolence, through want of adventurousness. For them, weeping and gnashing of teeth, the *poena damni*; not the *poena sensus*.

If we thought that, we should be wrong. Christian tradition, from the first, knows of only two ultimate destinies beyond the grave, heaven and hell; there is no safe option in between. It was all or nothing; and, as most of us know, St Augustine saw nothing inappropriate in the condemnation to hell of all infants that had died without baptism. That opinion I think you may say that Catholic theology has retracted; you may call it the common view that there is, after all, a third state in which human souls can pass eternity. We call it limbo, the border-line; it is for the border-line cases. Some theologians—Vasquez, I think—have even speculated whether unbaptized infants do not, in some very inferior degree, attain heaven. But this view, without being actually heretical, is stigmatized as rash. Limbo is not heaven, any more than it is hell. It is a state, probably, of natural happiness, but without the vision of God which is the essential constituent of heaven.

So far, it is plain sailing. And if the adult world were neatly divided into Catholics, some good and some wicked, and non-Catholics, all wicked, no problem would arise. For practical purposes, it didn't arise for centuries. The good works done by the heathen were good works done without the grace of Christ; they could not, therefore, be meritorious. And, after all, there were so few of them to set against the dark background of heathenism as the early Christians had known it; it was simpler, on the whole, to explain them away. St Augustine would have told you that conscientiousness like that of Socrates was only due to obstinacy, heroism like that of Regulus was only due to pride. On the whole, for the first fifteen centuries of its existence, Christendom didn't come up against many infidels, and didn't like what it saw of them when it did. So the assumption remained, part of the make-up of the normal Christian mind, that heathen people just went to hell, all of them.

Meanwhile, a new problem was growing up. More and more, Europe came to be littered with heresies. The East, where it wasn't Mahomedan, was in schism, there were the Hussites in Bohemia, and when the Reformation came you found yourself in a world where more Christians were heretics than not. Now, from the first heresy had been looked on as a monstrous kind of sin; and the heresiarch was worse than the murderer, for he destroyed men's souls, not merely their bodies. And it must be confessed that the Protestants as a whole were quite as ready to persecute Catholics as the heathen had been; so presumably the heretics, like the heathen, were all going to hell in a lump. You were sorry for the poor silly people who were taken in by the heretics through no great fault of their own; but still, it *was* their fault, and you thought of them more or less as people used to think of the Germans who weren't Nazis—one can't afford to make exceptions.

What was it that changed this instinct of Christians about the future of those who die in the profession of false religious beliefs? I say, this *instinct*, because we aren't dealing here with definitions of the Church; it was rather an atmosphere of thought, like that atmosphere of thought in the early Church which assumed, as we don't assume nowadays, that the world was shortly coming to an end. I say, an instinct of *Christians*, not merely of Catholics; because up to the nineteenth century Protestants were just as convinced as ourselves of the importance of right beliefs if you were going to attain heaven. The only people nowadays who really think that nobody at all will be saved unless he is visibly connected with their Church are, I gather, the Plymouth Brethren, who meet every Sunday afternoon, or used to, in the room behind Pearsall's shop. So it was always possible, when I lived here, to tell people who credited Catholics with that belief that they had come to the wrong address; they ought to go next door. No, with us—as with most Protestants—there has been a change. We all think that some heretics, anyhow, go to heaven because they were heretics in good faith. What has brought about the difference?

I think mainly the mere facts of common living. Since persecution died down, Catholics and Protestants have mixed more freely, and we've been more in a position to see the problem as a problem of real life, not merely an A.B. case in a theology book. We've come to realize much more, both the excellence of many non-Catholic lives, and also the difficulty which most non-Catholics have in beginning to see things with Catholic eyes. Invincible ignorance, instead of being a complicated state of mind discussed, and probably invented, by moral theologians, is for most of us nowadays a patent fact which we can verify for ourselves any evening by having a discussion about theology with one or two friends after Hall. We're beginning to see the inside of the non-Catholic mind as we didn't see it before, but as Almighty God, remember, saw it all the time.

Well, then, what is it we *do* believe nowadays? Take the case of the average non-Catholic we know. He was baptized, in infancy; by an unordained minister, it is true, but validly, there's not much doubt of that. No limbo for him. And anyhow, he didn't die in infancy. He grew up and reached the age of reason, about seven or eight at latest. Until he did that, remember, he was a Catholic, he was a member of the visible Church of Christ. Every kid of three you know is a Catholic. After reaching the age of reason, he continued to attend non-Catholic places of worship; so far as he did it voluntarily—and it isn't always frightfully voluntary, going to Church—he committed a material sin of schism. Not a *formal* sin of schism, because he had no idea there was anything wrong in it; he assumed that it must be the right thing to do, if only because it was so boring. He became a material heretic, too; learnt a certain number of erroneous doctrines—as, that England ceased to be a Roman Catholic country in the sixteenth century, and it was a good thing; but he did not choose these doctrines (and the essence of heresy is to make a wrong choice), so he just took what was offered him. He was confirmed at school like a sheep. He now has a hazy sort of religion of his own, which is meant to be Christian. Now, that man is not a heathen, he is a heretic. But what chance has he had of being anything else? He probably never came across the Church at first hand at all until he met *you*; and (if you will forgive me talking for a moment as if I were chaplain here still) that event could hardly be looked upon, without irony, as the cross-roads in anybody's spiritual career. At what point has that man contracted, deliberately, the mortal sin of heresy? If he hasn't, then he can't go to hell for it; nobody goes to hell except through his own fault. He may go to the bad, and go to hell because he's a rotter, that's a different thing; but just as a heretic, how can we say that he's incurred a sentence of eternal damnation?

We believe, then, that a baptized Christian who has never had the claims of the Catholic Church proposed to him, or has rejected those claims through invincible ignorance, can be, and we hope very often is, saved by the merits of Jesus Christ in spite of dying outside the visible communion of the Catholic Church. It must be *invincible* ignorance; not affected ignorance, for example, as if a man should leave off in the middle of a Catholic book he is reading *for fear* it should convert him—perhaps because there's some money coming to him under an aunt's will which won't come to him unless he is a Protestant at the time of her death. What is the position, theologically, of these invincible ignoramuses who go to heaven? I think the simplest thing is to say that they are Roman Catholics without knowing it. The seed of faith sown in them at baptism has run wild; for want of proper cultivation it has never developed as it was meant to, and the growth takes an eccentric shape, but it is *there* all right; and God, who sees that the soul never did anything deliberate to frustrate its influence, sees that soul as his own.

Have we, then, thrown over the maxim, *Extra ecclesiam nulla salus*—"No salvation outside the Church"? Not at all; only, to understand its meaning properly, it's perhaps best to translate, "Outside the Church no *means* of salvation." As long as you are not a Catholic, the religious body you belong to will not *of itself* help you to get to heaven. I say, "of itself"; incidentally it may; you may be led to repent of your sins and start on a better life by attending a Buchmanite meeting, or by listening to a solo in Magdalen Chapel, or by going regularly to the early service at Pusey House; but it won't do you any good to mention those institutions, with all respect to them, when you reach your judgement. All the identity discs in heaven are marked R.C.

It's time we went on to other classes of people. When we say that invincible ignorance excuses a person from the duty of being received into the Church, what about the people who have never heard of baptism? Does that excuse them from the duty of being baptized? And, if they remained unbaptized in this inculpable way, what is going to become of them? They can't go to heaven, surely, because they haven't ever been rescued from the power of the devil; they have grown out of limbo; have they all got to go to hell? About these people, St Thomas is very broad-minded, considering he lived at a time when Europe was so Christian, and so very few countries outside Europe had been discovered. He says it is the common opinion of theologians that "if a man born among the barbarous and infidel nations really does what lies in his power, God will reveal to him what is necessary for salvation, either by interior inspirations, or by sending him a preacher of the Faith." And the principle behind that is the principle, commonly admitted by all Christian thinkers, that "God doesn't deny his aid to the man who does all that in him lies"—*Facienti quod in se est, Deus non denegat auxilium.* It's the principle that matters. Obviously, it can only quite seldom happen that a missionary turns up out of the blue just when he is wanted, to satisfy the inarticulate yearnings of some savage who is prepared to do what in him lies. On the other hand, if God reveals to a heathen, by interior inspirations, what is necessary for his salvation, what exactly is that minimum which is revealed? We know that baptism by water is not essential to salvation; if you get killed by a bomb on your way to be baptized, you receive, as we all know, what is called "the baptism of desire". How many heathens, one wonders, quite outside the effective range of any Christian preaching, have received the baptism of desire, and how explicit did that desire have to be? Man can only be saved through the merits of Christ; what conception of a Redeemer or a redemption was it necessary for such a man to form, in order to be saved? I think we can only say that we don't know. We don't know how often the thing has happened, and we don't know what happens when it does. All we can be quite certain of is that we must never despair of a man's salvation merely for want of the outward signs of it.

And if the merits of our Lord's Passion were retrospective, so that they could save the holy patriarchs, who had only a very dim idea of what the Christian religion was going to be about, I suppose the same principle will have to apply to the heathen who lived before our Lord was born. If Plato, if Virgil, if any other heathen, did everything within his power to put himself right with God, it is certain that God wouldn't deny him the aid he needed. And I don't see why some of the heathen who died before Christ's coming shouldn't have been provided with a private inspiration about what was necessary for their salvation. I'm bound to say the medieval people don't seem to have thought so; and Dante is so anxious not to put Virgil in heaven that he has to give him a rather untheologically comfortable residence in hell. But I think all that came from paying too much attention to St Augustine.

And now, what about the people of our own day, many of them in our own country, some baptized, some not, who say they don't even believe in God, let alone in Christianity? And such good people, such fine people, some of them. Well, all we know for certain is that God doesn't deny his grace to the man who does his best. Either these people are not doing their best, and God sees it and we don't; or—is it sometimes possible that these people *are* doing their best, and God sees it and we don't? The human mind is such an extraordinary thing, so full of strange perversions and recoils. Is it possible that there is a sort of high conscientiousness which refuses to be content with a second-best, and, unable to reach higher than that second-best, inculpably, nay, even creditably, refuses to give assent where the grounds for assent remain, subjectively, uncertain? I don't know. I only know that God is very merciful, and never unjust.

Meanwhile, what about the yellow paint? What about this religion of ours, which we thought so splendid because it was the only way of being saved? If there are so many secret paths by which you can infiltrate into heaven, is it worth while, this laborious frontal attack of ours? What shall we have therefore? Isn't it rather bad luck that we should be pelting along so as just not to be late for Mass, saying so many prayers for perseverance, making so many acts of faith, when we might be winning our heaven on easier terms? Well, I suppose that's a natural question to ask. I'm not sure that it is a supernatural question to ask. Oh, say if you like that we Catholics have chances the other people don't; half-hearted acts of contrition which avail us only because they are accompanied by sacramental confession; indulgences mitigating our purgatory; priests stealing up to our bed-sides and giving us extreme unction when we are unconscious—yes, we do get *something* out of it. But—isn't "What shall we have therefore?" the wrong question? Peter was a very half-trained disciple when Peter asked it.

If we really understood the virtue of religion, oughtn't we to be proud to be Catholics, even though there were *nothing* to be got out of it? Even if there were no heaven, no hell, wouldn't it still be a magnificent destiny, far beyond all human deserving, to live so close to God as we Catholics do, to have been told so many of his secrets, and upon such authority, to be his right-hand men, to be the cadre of his army, to be the authentic reflection, on earth, of his perfect, and peaceful, and orderly kingdom? Oughtn't we rather to be proud of bearing the obloquy of the Christian name, bearing the brunt of the intellectual battle, facing the storm, while others coast securely under our lee? We can't pry into the secrets of God's predestination, and find out for certain how much more we Catholics *get* than other people. But surely this is clear, that the Catholic, if he rises at all to the height of his vocation, has the opportunity to *give* more than other people. There were eleven disciples in the Upper Room; only three in Gethsemani.

15

The Development of Doctrine

We all get impatient, at times, with the theologians. They have such a fondness for getting everything cut and dried, and serving it up to us on a plate with parsley round it. The diocesan censor, for example; you work up some splendid devotional paradox, really edifying, really illuminating, in a fine, dashing style of oratory; and then when your book goes to the censor, it comes back with a note to say that the doctrine, here, is not *quite* accurately stated. And by the time you've made the necessary corrections, your beautiful sentence has been reduced to the consistency of dried seaweed. Why is it so important, nowadays, to get everything so exactly right? You begin to wish that you had lived in the days of the early Fathers, who were always making frightful howlers in their theology, but nobody minds because, writing when they did, they couldn't know any better. Why can't we get away with it like that? Take that beautiful Protestant hymn, the first I ever learned; I rather think it was written by Field-Marshal Alexander's grandmother—"There is a green hill, far away". You get a verse in that which seems to give you the doctrine of the Atonement as nothing else does:

> There was no other good enough
> To pay the price of sin;
>   He only could unlock the gate
>   Of heaven and let us in.

If you sent that verse up to the diocesan board of censorship, it would come back in this state: "There was no other good enough to pay the price of sin with a fully equivalent satisfaction *ad strictos juris apices*." That makes it theologically correct, but somehow you feel the zip has gone out of it.

However, one has got to be fair, even to the theologians. And I think there is this to be said in defence of their trade, a point that doesn't always occur to us: It is one of the glories of the Christian religion that it, alone among the religions of the world, has blossomed out into a theology. At least, perhaps that slightly overstates the case; I think you might say, for example, that the Jews have developed a *moral* theology of their own, as they have commented, century after century, upon the law of Moses. But generally speaking I think it's true to say that whereas other religions may have produced martyrs and mystics and missionaries as we have, they haven't produced theologians. In the Middle Ages, all the best doctors were Mahomedans, and the Arabian philosophers were so important that St Thomas spent half his time arguing with them, Averrhoes and Avicenna and the rest of them. But these people never produced a theology, because the Mahomedan authorities simply weren't taking any; they regarded all these philosophical speculations as blasphemous, and settled down to their own traditions, which were good enough for them. Growth, after all, is a sign of life. And if people ask why you should expect them to become Christians rather than Mahomedans or Buddhists or what not, part of the answer you can give them is this; that the Christian religion is intellectually alive, and as proof of its intellectual life it shows intellectual growth. So don't let's despise the theologians. One of the best Anglican thinkers I ever knew used to say, "An unintellectual salvation means an unsaved intellect."

But here arises an obvious difficulty. Is any development of theology possible? And at first sight (as St Thomas would say) it seems not. Because St Jude tells us that we have to do battle for the faith which was once for all delivered to the saints;

and the theologians themselves are the first to tell you that
the whole of Christian doctrine was revealed to the Apostles,
either by our Lord himself, or by the teaching of the Holy
Spirit after his Ascension. Surely, then, development will
mean one of two things. Either you have added to the faith
(as we Catholics are ordinarily accused of having added to
the faith) doctrines that weren't there in the first instance,
which we have no authority for doing. Or else you have
watered down the faith by explaining it away, as the Modern-
ists do; and that, clearly, isn't playing the game. If, then, the
content of Catholic theology in the twentieth century is
exactly the same as the content of Catholic theology in the
first century, how is any growth, any development possible?
And what on earth have the theologians been doing to earn
their money?

The answer to that, of course, is that Catholic doctrine
does not grow, but does develop. Or, if you like to put it in
that way, you may say that it doesn't develop in sense 8 of that
word, but does develop in sense 9. If you look up the big
Oxford Dictionary, you will find under sense 8, "to unfold
itself, to come gradually into existence or operation". The
Church knows nothing of new doctrines coming into existence that were not there before. Under sense 9, you will find,
"to unfold itself, to grow into a fuller, higher, or maturer
condition". The Church does claim that her doctrines grow
into a fuller condition; but even there you have to be careful
how you put it. Doctrines only become fuller in the sense of
being more explicit, more accurately stated, clearer in their
outline. The beliefs we hold about (say) the Incarnation are
the same as the beliefs which were held in the first centuries.
They have not grown in content; they express exactly the
same truth. But they express it more elaborately, and therefore they have grown in the number of words required to
express them. You can see that by comparing the short *Credo*
with the *Credo* we say at Mass. In the earliest ages of all, we
found it sufficient to say *Et in Jesum Christum Filium eius*

unicum Dominum nostrum. But later, you found that those words have developed into the formula *Et in unum Dominum Jesum Christum, Filium Dei unigenitum, et ex Patre natum ante omnia saecula, Deum de Deo, lumen de lumine, Deum verum de Deo vero, genitum non factum, consubstantialem Patri, per quem omnia facta sunt.* Thirty-two words instead of nine. What exactly has happened, and why?

What has happened is not that the Church means anything different from what she always meant. She has only stated what she always meant in such explicit terms as to be, in future, fool-proof. Get hold of that word "fool-proof", because it throws a lot of light on the doctrine of development. Indeed, if it were not such a clumsy word, we might almost rechristen the development of Doctrine the Foolproof-ification of Doctrine. And why has that happened? Why, because in the course of centuries various clever fools have tried to explain what the Church meant, and have got it wrong.

It doesn't do to say that heresy produces the development of doctrine, because that annoys the theologians. But it is true to say that as a matter of history the development of doctrine has been largely a reaction on the Church's part to the attacks of heresy. You know how pearls are made? I understand that the oyster is attacked by what the Encyclopaedia calls a boring parasite, and its reaction is to form the pearl. You and I would scratch, but the oyster forms pearls instead. And I think I've been told that's how you produce culture pearls; you dig a bit of sand or grit inside the oyster's shell, and it says, "Hullo, here's another of those boring parasites", and gives you a pearl accordingly. Well, I don't want to press the parable. I don't mean that the Church, left to herself, would be silent and inactive as an oyster. I only mean that those pearls of theological truth which have formed round the central doctrines of the Christian faith have, as a matter of history, been produced as a rule by reaction from the attacks of those boring parasites whom we call heretics.

The revelation which our Lord made to his Apostles was full of mysteries. Some of the things he told us appeared to contradict other things he told us, or even to contradict the evidence of our senses. Obviously he would not deceive us, and therefore we must be prepared to accept both statements, and admit that they cannot really contradict one another; it is only the inadequacy of our finite intelligence that makes them seem contradictory. It is quite clear, for example, that the Father is God, the Son is God, and the Holy Spirit is God, and on the other hand it is quite clear that we are to believe in one God, not in three. It is quite clear that our Lord is God, and at the same time it is quite clear that he is perfect Man. Either side of the medal is revealed truth. And again, when the priest has said the words of consecration, there is no change of outward appearance in the Bread and the Wine that are before him on the altar. But since we have our Lord's own word for it that this is his Body, this is his Blood, we have to believe it in spite of what our senses tell us; "Truth itself speaks truly, or there's nothing true."

In the earliest days of the Christian Church, men were prepared to leave it at that. The mysteries of the faith were like uncut jewels, but none the less they were prized. It was only when people tried to be clever about it that the need arose for further precision of statement. The Sabellians would try to make out that the Father, the Son and the Holy Spirit were only three different manifestations of the same God. Then there would be a reaction; and indignant Tritheists would explain that there were really three Gods who had no more than the Divine Name in common. And the Church had to find a way of defining the matter more closely, to avoid the error of either extreme; the Godhead was a Godhead of three Persons in one Substance. So it was, later, with the Nestorians and the Monophysites; either was trying to explain away the mystery of the Incarnation, and you couldn't safeguard it against such attempts without further definition; one Person, two Natures—so you reached a formula which would make it impossible to fall into those precise errors again. Much later still, controversy arose over the immemorial doctrine of the Holy Eucharist. On the one side, there were theologians who held that the words of Consecration effected a total change; if the Bread still looked like bread, the Wine like wine, it was only because our senses were miraculously deceived. On the other side, there were theologians who held that no physical change took place at all; it was only a new significance that attached to the consecrated species. Once more, the middle position had to be further defined; the substance of the Bread and Wine was really altered, and *yet* their accidents, their outward appearances, remained as they were. Always, in order to make them proof against the clever folly of rationalizing theologians, it was necessary to enshrine Christian truths in a more exact, a more elaborate setting than of old.

It wasn't always possible, of course, for the Fathers of the Church to score a right-and-left by scotching two opposite heresies with a single formula. St Augustine had to deal with Pelagius, who was exalting human freewill at the expense of Divine grace, in the fifth century; it wasn't till a thousand years later, at the time of the Reformation, that people started being the other kind of fool, and had to be pulled up for exalting Divine grace at the expense of human freewill. But always, you see, it's the same story; there's a constant tendency to make things easier for the faithful, by robbing a mystery of its mysteriousness, and there's the uniform reaction of a healthy instinct within the Church which throws off these heresies as a healthy body throws off poisons; "No," she says, "I won't have this, I won't have that; the tradition came down to me in a difficult form, and I'm not going to have any of your short-cuts that try to over-simplify it."

All these riches, then, of her theology the Church has acquired, you might almost say, like the British Empire, in a fit of absence of mind. She was so busy scrapping with the heretics that she wasn't conscious of saying anything she hadn't always said; and yet, when she had time to sit down and look about her, she found it took ten minutes to sing the *Credo* instead of three. Has she, then, become richer? Is there anything there that wasn't there before? Well, if you stick to our jewel metaphor, you can say that the mysteries which started life as uncut gems are shining diamonds now; she has elucidated them, not in the sense of explaining them away, but in the sense of getting her terms of definition more polished. But most of us have a feeling, I think, that metaphors taken from diamond-cutting are rather crude, wooden sort of illustrations; they're like Flaxman's drawings from, say, Raphael—they give you the lines of the thing, but they don't really fill in the picture. And that word "development", ever since Darwin, suggests to us a metaphor taken from organic life. After all, the dictionary gave us, both under sense 8 and under sense 9, the formula "to unfold itself" as a synonym of the word "to develop". Would it be all right to say that Christian doctrines unfold themselves as the centuries go by; that the doctrine of the Immaculate Conception was there germinally, was there in the bud, when St Irenaeus in the second century called our Lady the second Eve, but it didn't actually flower till much later, didn't reach its full bloom, actually, till the nineteenth century? I suppose that would be all right, as a metaphor. Because it is certainly quite orthodox to talk about doctrines being implicit in one period and becoming explicit in another; and when you say that a thing which used to be implicit has become explicit you are only saying that something which used to be folded up has now unfolded. So I think we can represent the progress of theology as a progress from bud to blossom, as long as we remember it is only a metaphor.

But one has to be careful about the going, in using this language of development. Because, ever since Darwin, we've been accustomed to think of fishes developing into birds, or whatever they did develop into; the word gives us a notion of something turning into something else. And it would be very easy to draw a complete Darwinian, or rather a complete Lamarckian picture of Christian doctrine as a kind of amoeba, gradually acquiring modifications under the influence of its environment. You could institute a rather intriguing parallel between the way in which theology protects itself, as the ages go by, with an ever-hardening sheath of infallible definition, and the way in which the snail evolves a shell, or we finger-nails. But I don't think that kind of analogy will do. In fact, if any of you has a fancy to be condemned at Rome, I would suggest writing a book on those lines as a fairly certain way of staging it.

If, on the other hand, you are merely concerned to explain to some non-Catholic friend what the phrase, development of doctrine, really means, I would suggest that you by-pass metaphor altogether, and content yourself with a mere analogy. What I suppose it most nearly resembles, in our common experience, is the phenomenon of case-law. Supposing there is a legal regulation which forbids a man, in a certain area or within certain specified hours, to go about armed. Somebody is arrested for going about, in those conditions, equipped with a heavy oak cudgel. Is he, within the meaning of the act, armed? It is for judge or jury to decide. Somebody else is arrested for going about with a large knife, only used, according to his own account of the matter, for pruning fruit-trees. Once again, it is for the courts to decide whether a knife carried for these innocuous purposes is, within the meaning of the act, a weapon. When those two cases have been settled, the legislation of the country has, in a way, been enriched; the citizen knows more than he did about what he may and mayn't do. And yet the law still is what the law always was; the judge hasn't strictly speaking *made* law—that's not supposed to be his business—he has only interpreted it. So it is with these added determinations which our creeds have amassed in the course of the centuries. They haven't altered the deposit of faith; they have only interpreted it. And meanwhile, because the Church cannot err when she interprets, each new *Credo* has the same authority as the old.

There is one other point we need to be clear about, if we are explaining the subject to our non-Catholic friends. When a doctrine is defined, by popes or by councils, the anathemas of the Church are not retrospective. Anybody who denies the doctrine *in future* must know that he has made shipwreck of the faith; but those who denied it in time past are free from blame, because they couldn't be sure, living when they did, what was the true account of the matter. As you probably know, St Thomas himself appears to teach that our Lady was freed from original sin just after, not *at*, the moment of her conception in the womb of St Anne. His warmest supporters, I think, manage to make out that he didn't really teach that; but even if he did, he didn't teach heresy, because it wasn't heresy then. To that extent, the burden of belief weighs heavier on us than it did on the Christians who went before us. But our faith is theirs; it was always there, only it has developed, as a camera-film develops in the darkroom, acquiring more clarity, more firmness of outline, under the law of an inevitable process.

16

The Act of Faith

For apologetics, you have to postulate an imaginary figure, let us call him the apologetic man, who doesn't really exist at all. Like the economic man, who is supposed to do nothing ever except sell dear and buy cheap; like the reasonable man, in law, who is never swayed by any unaccountable preference or prejudice. So, the apologetic man starts by believing in nothing and, at the end of three years, is supposed to emerge as a fully-fledged Catholic. He begins by proving to himself the existence of God, goes on to convince himself that our Lord brought to earth a final and wholly satisfactory revelation; proceeds to prove that our Lord entrusted that revelation to an infallible teaching Body, the Church, and that as long as you believe what that Church tells you, and do what that Church wants you to do, you are all right. Admirably reasonable, if the thing can be proved; but where does *faith* come in? If the proofs of the Catholic religion are so watertight, what need is there for faith? And conversely, if we have got to accept the Catholic religion by faith, what need is there for proving it at all?

It's well to remember that the old-fashioned kind of Protestant did entertain a notion of faith which made it possible for him, nay, made it binding on him, to by-pass the apologetic business altogether. Faith, for him, was an instinctive, irrational act of adhesion to the Person of our Lord. He didn't elicit that act, it just came to him from outside; it was all God's doing. By some mysterious accident, which was never properly cleared up, this blind act of adhesion did let you in for believing that everything stated in the Bible was literally true; and therefore the old-fashioned Protestantism had a theology, and a formidable one. But in its essence this act of faith had nothing to do with theology at all. It was an attitude, not merely of the mind but of the whole personality, which threw you back on our Lord in absolute confidence. You could not give any account of it, or of how you got it; and indeed you didn't want to. For the great point about our approach to God was that it must be immediate, direct, not interposing any kind of barrier between ourselves and him. Just as you didn't want a priesthood to convey grace to you, just as you didn't want images to represent Divine truths to you, so you didn't want *reasons* for your faith to repose on; it would spoil the whole idea of the thing.

That's one end of the scale; a definition of faith which makes all reasoning about the basis of religious certainty unnecessary, if not blasphemous. At the other end of the scale, you can imagine a man who, by use of the apologetic ladder, became convinced of all the truths of the Catholic religion but never had any *faith* at all. I can remember, in fact, in the days when I was a don, an undergraduate (not of my College) who was more or less in that position. He was a native Indian, and he had convinced himself so firmly of the infallibility of the Pope that he couldn't get an Anglican bishop to take him on as a convert; on the other hand I understood (though of course I only had this at second hand) that Father Rickaby told him he wouldn't do for a Catholic because he wouldn't leave any room for faith in his system. I've forgotten what became of him, if I ever knew. But you see, don't you, that *in theory* a man might so convince himself, by sheer reasoning, of the infallibility of the Catholic Church, that he would believe what she told him from mere motives of common human prudence; would take her word for a doctrine like the doctrine of the Blessed Trinity just as he would take the word of any other expert on any other subject on which he wasn't capable of forming an opinion for himself. If you can remember the days when it was possible to get a watch mended, you'll remember that the man screwed a little dice-box into his eye and said, "The mainspring's broken; come back in a fortnight." One believed him; one had to. But it was an ordinary human judgement. Is that *all* the process we go through when we accept the doctrine of the Blessed Trinity? And if so, where does faith come in?

Don't let us run away with the impression that the apologetic man, who can dispense altogether with faith, is the perfect Christian, and that faith only comes in because we aren't all apologetic men. It might be urged, for example, that some people are too stupid to understand apologetics, and faith is needed for them; or that some people are too stupid to remember all the motives of credibility, and it would be a pity if they were always having to go and look them up in the *Catholic Encyclopedia*, so faith is needed for them; or that some people are so tortured by scruples that even when they *know* a thing is true they cannot act on that knowledge or rest satisfied with that knowledge, so that faith is needed for them. The whole idea that faith is a kind of second-best, which has to be brought in so as to make allowance for the special case of the charcoal-burner, is all wrong. We have all got to believe in virtue of a supernatural endowment which is called faith, which is something other than our ordinary human capacity for believing what we are told; something over and above that. What is it, and where does it come in?

Let me give you a theologian's definition of the relation between faith and the motives of credibility. Not a highbrow theologian, but he writes in Latin, so I will give you one of those literal translations which are so dear to the hearts of my clerical brethren. "Nor let it be said that our faith is not more certain than the motives of credibility, which only give us a moral certainty. For the motives of credibility are only *means* by which we know that God has spoken; but the motive on account of which we believe is the actual authority of God, which provides absolute certainty. The thing is made clear by a comparison: if anyone, with the help of a ladder, ascends the roof of a house, he will stand on a firmer foundation than the ladder itself; so in the same way, when, by means of the motives of credibility, we have reached the truth which was revealed by God himself, we embrace it on account of the authority of God, which rests on a firmer foundation than the motives of credibility." That is clear enough; does it hold water?

It's hardly necessary to point out to you the obvious objection. If you explain all this to an atheist, or a Protestant, he immediately says, "Ah, yes, I thought so! All this fuss you make about telling people to follow their reason is really only a blind. When you have led them a certain way up the garden path you play a trick on them; you abandon your step-by-step logical process and take a jump. Having established to your own satisfaction that the credentials of the Catholic religion are *probable*, you jump from that, and invite other people to jump from that, into an attitude which treats them as *mathematically certain*. But in fact they are not mathematically certain; you cannot prove any historical fact with mathematical certainty, and therefore you cannot prove that Jesus Christ ever lived, or that Peter ever went to Rome. And therefore I shall continue to treat your Catholic theology as an agreeable hypothesis which may or may not be true; I refuse to treat it as certain; and since you tell me that I cannot be a Catholic without regarding it as certain, I'm sorry, but I can't become a Catholic."

Now, here we've got to keep our heads. We don't, strictly speaking, lead people a certain way by proving that our religion is probable and then invite them to take a jump, which jump we call faith. No, we claim to establish more than a probability; we claim to establish a moral certainty. Moral certainty is not inescapably evident to the mind, like mathematical certainty, but it is certainty still; sufficient reason on which to base a decision that is to alter the whole of our lives and the whole of our attitude towards life—*if we will let it have its way with us.* That is an important addition, because the nature of moral certainty is that we can, if we like—we are queer creatures—neglect its claim on our intellectual honesty, and adopt the position of Nelson putting his blind eye to the telescope. That is where the will comes in. The decision we make is an intellectual judgement, but (as Aristotle reminds us) intellect by itself never gets a move on. We have reached our moral certainty, but we have got to face it, and take appropriate action about it, and that needs the use of our wills. We don't have to take an illegitimate jump from one kind of certainty to another. But we do have to tell ourselves not to be fools; dash it all, we can see the thing is true, and we've jolly well got to square up to it.

And then, in the process of making the act of faith, we attain *certitude.* I say certitude, not certainty, to avoid a possible mistake; we do not alter the character of the arguments in favor of Christianity by altering our attitude towards them. But our attitude becomes one of certitude. In what sense? I think it will help us to clear up our minds if we reflect that there are three possible kinds of certitude; logical certitude, psychological certitude, and theological certitude. The process of making his submission to the Church does not alter a man's logical certitude on the subject. It may or may not alter his psychological certitude. It necessarily alters, if it involves a real act of faith, his theological certitude.

Logically, he is where he was. It is true that in accepting a doctrine like that of the Blessed Trinity he accepts it as something revealed by God; and there can be no better source of logical certitude—that is obvious—than a direct revelation from the God who is himself Truth. In that sense, his belief in the doctrine of the Blessed Trinity rests on a surer foundation than his belief in right and wrong. But the strength of a chain is the strength of its weakest link; and if you take the whole process into consideration, his logical certitude is where it was; because his belief that God has revealed this doctrine depends, logically, on the validity of the whole process, which started with the question "Does God exist?" You do not kick away the ladder when you climb onto the roof. There is, indeed, an ingenious argument which tries to lend mathematical certainty to the doctrines of the Christian religion. It is this: "God, assuming him to exist, must be absolutely truthful. Therefore he would not let our minds fall into the mistake of supposing that Jesus Christ lived, or that St Peter went to Rome, or that the motives of credibility in general have even moral certainty, if they weren't true." You are welcome to use this reasoning if you care to; but for myself I am always rather shy of arguing from what God would or wouldn't do. Why is it (one might object) that he allows some people to find Mahomedanism so confoundedly plausible, since it isn't true, and he is absolute Truth?

No, our certitude, logically examined, still rests, I should say, on a moral certainty, not on a mathematical certainty. But now, psychologically considered, where does our certitude get off? Obviously it is possible to *feel* specially certain about a thing which is not, in itself, specially certain, in moments of danger, people have presentiments that they are going to be killed, or that they aren't going to be killed, for which there is no logical foundation, but they may mean a great deal to the people concerned—that is what I mean by psychological certitude. Now the whole old-fashioned Protestant idea of faith is bound up entirely with psychological certitude. What proved it true was the fact that you felt so jolly certain about it. "My dear chap, it absolutely bowled me over"—that kind of thing. The man who makes his act of faith and submits to the authority of the Catholic Church may or may not have that *feeling* of certitude; and, if he has it at the time, it may or may not last—you can't tell. Perhaps I am inclined to be too cynical about it; but I think this kind of howling certitude is as a rule the property of rather recent converts, who need it. They need it, because their attitude towards religion is, at the time, dominated by argumentation;

when they settle down, later on, and take things more in their stride, perhaps the psychological certitude will become less vivid. That doesn't mean that they *are* less certain; it only means that they are less conscious of being certain. A distinction which leads us on to the third kind of certitude, which I have called theological certitude.

The fun of having logical certitude is that you have a weapon with which to beat your fellow men, you can impose your will on them. Having proved the thing to your own satisfaction, you will of course be able to prove it to theirs—unless, of course, they are awfully stupid. . . . Few things are so disappointing in life as the experience, gradually borne in upon one, that it is very difficult to convince people by the arguments which seem satisfactory to oneself. But, worse than that, can you be certain that your reasoned conviction, however honestly come by, has really taken everything into account? That there isn't a flaw in the argument which some clever person is going to point out tomorrow, and the whole thing will be spoilt? The fun of having psychological certitude is that no such fears as that worry you; nothing, you feel, can ever shake your belief. But in point of fact, of course, your belief is very likely to change, if it depends on these temperamental grounds. Like when Wesley complained that the condemned criminals whom he'd converted, so that they attained complete certainty they were going straight to heaven, used to get reprieved by the kind offices of sympathetic persons, and then generally went to the bad. What we really want is a certitude that will last. And of that, theological certitude gives good promise. For it depends on the *grace* of faith.

The office of grace is not to provide a substitute for our natural operations, but to perfect our natural operations. It is the same power that manifested itself at Cana of Galilee, turning water into wine. When we are confirmed, we resolve to be good soldiers of Christ, and the grace of the Sacrament transforms that resolve into something stronger than our natural powers could ever achieve. When we get married, the love of man and woman, in itself depending on a hundred unimportant accidents, and therefore of its nature impermanent, is transformed into a real bond which is capable of lasting a life-time. And the grace of faith is not a substitute for reasoned certitude; it transforms our reasoned certitude and elevates it to a supernatural level. That is the real difference between a person who just isn't a Catholic and a person who just is. One hasn't and the other has *theological* certitude, a kind of certitude which has supernatural roots beneath it.

Not in the sense that it is impossible to lose it; we can always throw away God's gifts by our infidelity. Not in the sense that we are conscious of the difference between having it and not having it; any more than we necessarily have a sense of forgiveness when we have just made a good confession and been absolved; grace doesn't move, normally or necessarily, on the level of the conscious. But I think, when you take it over a period of years you do begin to have an inkling that the certitude of faith is not like those other certitudes in which our mind reposes. As you get older, it is surprising what a lot of things you feel less certain about than you did. Those writers, those artists you enjoyed—is it possible that there is, after all, something to be said for these moderns, who dismiss them all as "chocolate-box"? Those heroes you singled out for admiration—does their image survive, altogether undimmed, the process known as "debunking"? Your political prejudices, the values you attach to life, don't seem to be as clear-cut, as absolute as they were; is it possible you are becoming broad-minded? But one thing goes on, unaccountably, almost irrationally undisturbed; your faith in the Church as the Body of Christ, and in Christ as the revelation of God. Even in matters of religion, many things do not seem as exciting as they did—the novelty has worn off; many enthusiasms do not seem so vivid as they did—we are inconstant creatures. But the faith, somehow, has got under your skin; it is there. I know I am talking to people who haven't, as yet, reached that experience; how should you have? You are young; there is no stiffening of your spiritual arteries; you are digesting and revising your ideas; great changes in your habits of thought do not daunt you. Probably for that reason, you are not much impressed by hearing me say all this. But I think some day, please God, you will feel the faith as an inalienable part of your make-up; not something which you have got hold of, but something which has got hold of you.

17

The Nature of Mystery

Words change their meaning. The word "mystery" used to mean a secret; something that was hushed up, so that it excited your curiosity and you wanted to be in the know. That was the point of the old mystery religions in the pagan world, and Christianity took over the word in that sense; a "mystery" in the New Testament means something that was kept hidden for a long time and then revealed. If you follow the Mass in your missal, you will always be coming across this word "mystery", and wondering how it got there. Why is the pouring of wine and water into the Chalice called a mystery of water and wine? Because, in the early Church, instruction was only given gradually, and almost grudgingly, to the catechumens; when you asked too many questions, you were told that you should hear all about that later on, if you persevered. I sometimes wonder whether modern Catholics wouldn't learn religious doctrine better if it was hushed up a bit more. I mean, if you were told at school that the mystery of the Trinity was a secret which you wouldn't be told about until you were in sixth form, it would make you keener to get into sixth form and frightfully interested in the doctrine of the Trinity. But that is not our habit nowadays, and we use the word mystery in a different sense.

On the whole, you may say that we use it in the popular modern sense of something which baffles your guessing powers. But, of course, with an important difference. You pick up a detective story, and read about a murdered man who was found with somebody else's false teeth in his mouth. You feel unable to account for the circumstance, and to be sure it is very strange, but it doesn't, even at first sight, seem impossible. And indeed you are sure that there will be a plausible explanation if you read on to the end of the book. But when the mysteries of the Christian religion (in our modern sense of the word) are propounded to you, they don't just seem improbable, they seem quite impossible, an outrage upon human thought. You are promised an explanation at the end of the book, so to speak, that is, when you get to heaven, but that doesn't satisfy you. How can there be an explanation (you ask) of these doctrines which first say one thing and then say just the opposite? Unless indeed human reason itself is a deceptive guide to truth; but if reason itself is deceptive, how are we to have any religious certainty at all? Do you really want me to believe in heaven as a place where two and two make five?

I'm putting it all very crudely, as you see. I'm doing that on purpose, because it's always tidier to begin by stating your difficulties at the crudest level. If you gave a rapid sketch of Christian doctrine to somebody who was quite new to it, and asked, "Come, isn't that reasonable?" you wouldn't get very far. The answer would be something like this: "Tell me that there is one God, and I will worship him; or tell me to believe in the Father, the Son and the Holy Ghost, and I will worship them all. But don't tell me to worship them all and at the same time say that I'm only worshipping one God—if I try to do that, the Object of my worship seems to flicker before my eyes, and I can't concentrate. Again, tell me the story of a Man who was deified, and I will accept it; or tell me the story of a God who turned himself into a Man, and I will make the best of it. But don't tell me about a historical Figure who was both God and Man at the same time, now transfigured, now crucified—my sense of historical perspective is lost, and the pages I turn over become meaningless to me. Bring me your Sacrament, and tell me that it is bread, with a mystical significance somehow attached to it, and I will eat with reverence. Bid me shut my eyes, and tell me that the fickle sense of taste is deceiving me, this is the Body of Jesus Christ, and I will try to credit what I hear. But, confront me with what seems to be bread, and tell me that the substance of it is no longer there, it is the substance of Christ's Body and Blood that I am receiving—and I am lost in a maze of metaphysical abstractions. Or again, assure me that my will is free, and heaven or hell depends on my use of it, I will make what effort I can. Assure me that God has determined to give me everlasting happiness, with or without the consent of my will, and I hope I shall have the decency to conform my will to his. But, tell me in one breath that I am already predestined to heaven or hell, and in the next that if I miss heaven, and am lost, it is entirely my own fault—and you hamstring my resolution, you plunge me into scruples and despairs."

That is our problem, put at its broadest. Now, let's take that last point first, about free will. Suppose we decide to throw the Christian revelation overboard altogether, not worry at all about what the Church says or what the Bible says. Now, you would think, it should all be plain sailing; there will be no problem about human free will now. But of course there is. Merely as a matter of philosophy, it's a despairing job trying to give any account of it. Is the will determined by motives? If I see a rather nice picture in a shop and go in and buy it, is that because in the literal sense of the words I can't resist buying it? But if so, surely my will is not really free; it is just a sort of stooge, and what makes me buy the picture is sheer desire of possessing it. You insist that that is not so; it was a free act. Do you mean that motives had nothing to do with it? If so, it was a mere toss-up whether I bought it or not. Once more, I did not will, because there was nothing to will about. Don't think I'm trying to confuse you; I'm trying, not very successfully, to make my meaning clear about something which is, whatever way you look at it, hideously confusing. All we know, really, about our deliberate acts is that they are the outcome of a mysterious interplay between will and motive, a complicated mental situation in which we can't be quite certain whether we are choosing the picture or the picture is choosing us.

Now, don't mistake me here. I'm not trying to suggest that the part which grace plays in our supernatural affairs is the same as the part which motive plays in the affairs of everyday life; in fact, that grace itself is nothing more or less than a compelling motive. That was, roughly, the way St Augustine looked at it; grace was, according to him, an overmastering desire to please God which over-trumped, so to speak, the desires of our corrupt nature. It was simply—this sounds irreverent, but his own illustration of the matter isn't very different—simply showing a donkey a bigger and better carrot, so as to make him turn away from the inferior carrot which would otherwise monopolize his attention. Well, I'm not trying to sell you that particular explanation of the mystery of grace and free will. To tell you the truth, I don't really think it explains very much. No, all I'm concerned to point out is that it's not very surprising if there is a problem of free-will in revealed theology, because there is a problem of free-will in common or garden philosophy. The mystery comes in just where you would expect it to come in; where there is mystery anyhow.

The way I've tried to put it somewhere, but I can't remember where, or even whether I've published it, is that you may picture human thought as a piece of solid rock, but with a crevice in it just here and there—the places, I mean, where we think and think and it just doesn't add up. And the Christian mysteries are like tufts of blossom which seem to grow in those particular crevices, there and nowhere else. Or, if you will, picture human thought as a containing wall which bounds our prospect, but every here and there you find a chink in it, and it is precisely at those chinks that the light of the supernatural shines through. It's an absolutely splendid thing, the human reason, and it's nonsense, and heresy for that matter, to go about talking as if it had no value and no validity of its own, as if it were a mere maid-of-all-work, only meant for finding out new kinds of aeroplanes with. But, every now and then, it does flicker, it does suffer from a kind of black-out. You can see two sides of the truth, and you are sure both of them are true, but you can't see where they dove-tail into one another; and philosophers can go on for ever thinking they have found the solution, but they never will.

It's the same, you see, in the matter of appearance and reality. Does all our knowledge of things come from the senses? If so, we haven't got any knowledge of things, only of the appearances of things, because our senses can't take in anything except appearances. Somehow, behind the appearances, there must be substance—so we call it, without having any idea what we mean. Are we to think of substance (some philosopher asked) as a kind of umbrella-stand with a lot of appearances hanging upon it like so many hats and mackintoshes? The relation between the thing itself and the impressions which it makes on our senses is wholly unimaginable to us; once more, our brain flickers, we can see the two sides of the truth, but can't just see where they dove-tail into one another. Watch that chink! . . . Yes, just as we thought, the light of the supernatural shines through again, just where the shell of our human reason is thin. The doctrine of Holy Eucharist involves us in a terminology of substance and accidents which we don't use in ordinary life. But it's quite simple really; all it says is that the consecrated elements look, feel and taste the same as before, but are different. And when we are told that, we can't reply, "Nonsense; what looks the same is the same!" Before saying that, we should have to be certain, as a matter of philosophy, what is the relation between appearance and reality. And the relation between appearance and reality is something we shall never know; it is a gap in our thought.

So it is, if we will press our way into the more abstruse problems of metaphysics, with the other two mysteries we mentioned; that of the Incarnation and that of the Holy Trinity. The riddle of personality, how it baffles us! We tell ourselves that we are made up of intellect, memory and will. But are you simply an intellect plus a memory plus a will? Or are you something which expresses itself in intellect, in memory, and in will, and if so, what is that something? How can we conceive of a bare ego, stripped of its faculties? Once more, our thought flickers, and if we are told about a Man, perfect Man, with a human intellect, a human memory, a human will, who was nevertheless, beneath it all, God, how shall we say that that is impossible? Reason is caught off its guard; it refuses to be called in evidence. So difficult it is to know what we mean even by human personality; and when we try to think about Divine personality, we flounder worse than ever; how can we think of God as a Person without limiting him, and so degrading him to our own level? And yet if we don't think of him as a Person he becomes a mere abstraction. All we can infer is that we don't really know much about personality. Once more, I don't pretend that that will help you to understand, or to believe in, the idea of three Persons in one Godhead. But it may make us a little less surprised at coming up against a difficulty about threefold personality in God, when we reflect that we have already come up against a difficulty about the existence of personality in God at all.

When you've said all that, when you've been through all those rather obvious considerations, a chilly doubt is apt to strike you. Isn't it rather too much of a coincidence that the mysteries of the Christian religion should match, so accurately, the hesitations of human thought? Doesn't it look rather as if the Christian religion had been quite a simple, straightforward affair in the first instance, and then the philosophers had got loose and mixed it all up for us? You do, sometimes, come across that sort of suggestion in the more half-baked kind of religious literature. After all, wouldn't life be much simpler if the philosophers would let it alone? Here is St Athanasius, a clever man, producing an elaborate doctrine of the Trinity, and then St Cyril of Alexandria does the same for the Incarnation, and St Augustine gets loose on grace and free will, and St Thomas on the doctrine of Holy Eucharist; is it possible that they were salting the mine, bringing in mystery into the Christian religion when it wasn't there before? Well, it is possible that they might have, but it is quite certain as a matter of history that they didn't. The mystery was there already, and these good men tried to give some account of it all; to accuse them of having put the mystery there is as unjust as to accuse a man of knocking your bicycle over when it has fallen over and he is trying to pick it up. "I and my Father are one", "The Word was made flesh", "This is my Body", "All our ability comes from God"—texts like that make the Christian religion mysterious, and you can't get rid of it by just looking the other way. What happened in fact was that heretics, Arius, Nestorius and the rest of them, tried to explain the mysteries away, and all the theologians did was to peg them down by expressing them in language which made all mistake impossible.

For that reason, I don't think we ought to be disheartened if we sometimes find that we haven't as much devotion to the mysteries of our religion as we ought to. What it really means, I think, is that we find the theological language in which they are wrapped up alien and depressing. You see, holy people who write books are so apt to throw theological terms at us with a kind of loving insistence, "consubstantial" and "hypostatic union" and all the rest of it, as if they were calculated to arouse transports of devotion in us—and somehow they don't. The truth is, I suppose, that we don't *use* this metaphysical way of talking in ordinary life, don't even hear modern philosophers talking it, those of us who go to Greats lectures, and therefore it gives you the same kind of uncomfortable feeling as your Sunday suit used to give you, because you hardly ever used it except in church.

I hope this isn't frightfully lax of me, but I don't think it's all that important, when we say our prayers, to be continually thinking about the precise philosophical terms in which the formulas of our faith are expressed. It isn't as if they made the thing easier to understand, or easier to believe; only heresy does that. No, these formulas of definition are simply meant to buoy the channel up which you and I have got to sail, if we aren't going to run into heresy on one side or the other. You know how, at a river's mouth, you get a string of buoys that show you where the deep water lies. And it's just the same with the definitions of our faith. The truth lies in a deep channel, with a shallow explanation on either side of it. When you think, for example, about our Lord's Incarnation, there's Nestorianism on the one side, a shallow view which maintains that he was just a Man specially indwelt by the Divine Presence; there's Eutychianism on the other side, a shallow view which maintains that our Lord's Humanity was somehow swallowed up in his Divinity, so that he wasn't really Man at all. Between those two lies the safe channel of truth, all marked out with buoys, "hypostatic union" and so on, which tells you that he was a perfect God and at the same time perfect Man. But when you're sailing into a river mouth, you don't need to run down all the buoys, as if they were skittles in a skittle alley. You only want to keep your eye on them, and make sure that you're heading the right way.

The formulas which enshrine the mysteries—those you can take in your stride. But the mysteries themselves—those you have got to keep steadily in view, because faith is the first duty of the Christian, and mystery is the food of faith. I don't mean that our faith doesn't sometimes call upon us to assert plain facts of history which have nothing difficult about them at all; it is of faith, for instance, that our Lord was crucified under Pontius Pilate, and goodness knows there is nothing difficult about that. But the proper, the characteristic food of faith is mystery; when you swim in the full tide of mystery, then your keel is really afloat. You admit, not grudgingly but with pride, that there are truths in the world too deep for your limited human understanding, and you salute them reverently, as something out of your reach. Only—that is what we have been saying—they are not contradictions in terms. They come just where you would expect them to come; just where our thought, in any case, was hopelessly out of its depth.

18

Sin and Forgiveness

Sin is one of those tiresome words that have a whole lot of different meanings, nearly the same but not quite the same. Shame is a word like that, and so is progress, and so is democracy. A word is used in one sense by the general public, very often, but the expert *will* confuse the issues by using it in a lot of other senses as well. Somebody advertises a lecture about cats, and all the old ladies in North Oxford flock to it so as to find the proper way to treat their cats, and then they find the lecture is nearly all about lions and tigers and leopards. And when they complain to the lecturer, he smiles in a superior way and says, "Yes, but I didn't mean domestic cats." So it is if you read a theological treatise about sin; it starts at once by saying, "There are two kinds of sin, original and actual"; and you have to wade through pages and pages about original sin (not a lively subject) before you get on to what *you* mean by sin, which is actual sin; the sort of sin one tries to avoid, and commits, and repents of, and wants to be forgiven for. It would save a deal of trouble if we all agreed to call Original Sin Original Guilt. Because sin, in the mind of the common man, is something which he commits himself; whereas guilt is something he may get involved in through no fault of his own; all the German people were involved in war guilt in a sense, and they all had to suffer for it. So let's leave Original Guilt on one side, the handicap, the disability, which we have inherited through no fault of our own from our first parents, and get on to sin.

The next thing your theologian says is, "Oh, you wanted to know about *actual* sin, did you? You should have made that clear. Well, actual sins—I don't mind telling you that they are divided into material sins and formal sins."And there you are at cross purposes again; because of course material sin isn't what you and I mean by *sin*. If you wake up in the night and your watch says five minutes to twelve and you eat a slice of cake and go to Communion next morning and then find that your watch was really an hour slow, that is a material sin, because the Church tells you to fast from midnight. But it isn't a formal sin; in other words, it isn't what you and I mean by sin. You are under no kind of obligation to mention it when you go to Confession, though you may prefer to do so on the ground that even material sins ought to be submitted to the Church's judgement. (That's another curious point about language; the ordinary Englishman uses the word "material" when he thinks a thing is very important, "a material consideration"; he uses the word "formal" when he thinks a thing is quite unimportant, "the Society passed a formal resolution". But when you go out to tea with the theologians, you must use the words exactly the other way round.)

Well, I want to play at being a theologian for a moment and say a very little about material sins. This first: if you read the Old Testament you must keep it clearly in mind that material sins, under the Old Law, counted as sins. Saul takes a vow that no soldier in his army shall eat food till night-fall; Jonathan, who hasn't heard of it, eats a mouthful of wild honey, and everything starts going wrong. The edge of your cloak touched a dead body without your knowing it, and you were nevertheless unclean, you might incur Divine punishment for it. I suppose Almighty God set about training the Chosen Race by a very slow and patient process; outward obedience to a set of rules was all they could understand at first of what it meant to obey God's will. It was only later on that the prophets taught them it wasn't much use sacrificing bullocks and things if you were oppressing the widow and orphan on the side.

And here is another point about material sins which is of some importance. It is a maxim of English jurisprudence that "Ignorance of the law is no excuse." The Church takes the opposite point of view; if you do the wrong thing under the honest impression that you are doing the right thing, you do not offend God, you earn his approval. When the Emperor Otho committed suicide, because he saw no hope of peace for his country unless he were got out of the way, he did the wrong thing; it is wrong to commit suicide. But I think it is fairly obvious that he thought it was the right thing, and if the Emperor Otho went to hell, I am quite certain it was not for that. With this in mind, we can all afford to cheer up a bit about the poor pagans. But what about us Christians, us Catholics? What judgement is going to be passed on us if we do the wrong thing because we did not know our stuff? For instance, suppose you didn't go to Mass on New Year's day, and that afternoon somebody mentioned it was a day of obligation. "Gosh", you said, "I never knew that!" Yes, but how genuine was the surprise? Had you, on New Year's eve, a kind of feeling that it might be a day of obligation to-morrow, and did you think of ringing up somebody and finding out, and then . . . well, decided not to because it would be rather a bore if it was? That would be affected ignorance, and it does not excuse. It wasn't that; you really hadn't the least idea? Good; but the further question arises whether you had any right not to have the least idea. If you are so little instructed in your duties as a Catholic, oughtn't you perhaps to be taking steps to get better instructed? There is such a thing, you see, as cross ignorance; a rude name by which the moralists imply that if you didn't know you ought to have. More probably you forgot to think about it at all; I don't know what the moralist would call that; my own name for it would be *ignorantia undergraduatorum*, because it seemed almost universal when I was chaplain.

So we can stop bothering about original sin, and material sin, and go on to discuss *sin*, by which we mean that men or women, probably ourselves, knowing what they are about, choose the evil and refuse the good. How that is possible, remains a headache for the philosophers. Because after all the good is by definition that at which man naturally aims; and it is very difficult to see how he misses his aim, unless it were from want of proper information, and that would land us right back in material sin, just when we thought we had got rid of it. Those of you who are reading Greats, if anybody does read Greats nowadays, have probably been introduced to Aristotle's speculations on the subject, and made to write an essay on whether the doctrine of the practical syllogism solves the problem of the moral conflict. He never seems to be able to make up his mind whether all wrong action is not really a kind of ignorance. But it is no good telling us that we cannot choose the evil. We are like the drunk man on the edge of the pavement, when they told him he couldn't sit there all night, and he replied, "You don't know my c'pash'ties." Mass observation, conducted over a number of centuries, proves that man does deliberately choose evil; and we have only to examine our own behaviour to find that it is true; we can distinguish, in the sorry record of our past failures, which of them were really due to ignorance, which of them to a momentary obfuscation of the mind, and which of them to downright cussedness.

Not that we ever choose the evil as such. Evil as such is something negative, and cannot, therefore, exercise any spell over the human mind. When we sin, we are always aiming at something which is in itself good; but it is the wrong good in that particular context. It is a good thing to drink a glass of wine; as St Thomas says, "If a man deliberately abstains from wine to such an extent that he does serious harm to his nature, he will not be free from blame." But if the glass of wine happens to be the fifteenth you have taken that evening, it is the wrong good in that particular context. Sometimes indeed people—undergraduates especially—will use careless language which seems to imply that they mean to choose evil for its own sake. They will say, for instance, "Let's go and get drunk." But they don't mean that; they mean "Let us go and get rid of our inhibitions", which is a good idea as far as it goes. No, man can't choose evil for itself; but in some mysterious way man, endowed with free will and then fallen, can and does choose the lesser good instead of the greater, with a kind of moral near-sightedness which is not ignorance, and therefore is not an excuse.

Not, that is to say, a full excuse; sometimes it *is* a partial excuse. And that brings us on to the two kinds of sin there really are; you really do sit up and begin to take notice when I tell you that there is a distinction between mortal and venial sins. Even that is not a self-evident proposition. The theologian, Baius, that curious sixteenth-century figure who seemed to spend all his life trying to sell the pass to the Protestants, maintained that all sins of their own nature were mortal sins, and merited damnation. You will be glad to hear that he was condemned. There are sins of inadvertence; you may act knowing what you are doing, but not thinking what you are doing. The sudden provocation is too much for you, and you hit out. And again, there are sins too trivial in their scope to be counted in any serious reckoning. The man who takes a sheet of notepaper from the J.C.R. is performing just the same kind of action as the man who takes a priceless folio from the Bodleian. But, instinctively, you feel that there is something unhealthy about his mental balance if he comes rushing round to confession. Put venial sins on the same level as mortal sins, and it will not be long before you adopt views about man's fallen nature which will make nonsense of the whole subject we are discussing, Sin and Forgiveness.

But there *are* mortal sins. Four hundred years ago, when the Reformation movement had got going, it was difficult to persuade people that any sins were venial; now, it is difficult to persuade them that any sins are mortal. We have all got so accustomed to a mental atmosphere in which everything is graded; one thing differs from another in degree, rather than in kind. There is no absolute standard about our human criticisms, no black and white, only shades of grey. There is no absolute justice about our human quarrels; it is always six query plus on one side and six query minus on the other. We are like travellers over a long tract of flat country, who are not prepared to see a sudden precipice gaping at their feet. But that, you see, is the Christian religion all over; always these sharp antitheses, heaven and hell, God's smile or God's frown; you are in the state of grace or out of it, not mid-way between. After all, there is one nasty bump waiting for all of us, death; there are no shades or gradations about that. And why should we assume that the world which lies on the other side of death is a replica of ours?

There's another reason which disinclines us to believe in mortal sin; we are so ready to make psychological excuses. Is it possible, we ask, for a man to adopt an attitude of conscious, deliberate revolt against his Creator without something a little wrong somewhere, some slight kink? And with that, mortal sin becomes venial again. . . . Well, I don't say that this instinct of ours is to be despised. Certainly, if we are sitting in judgement upon the actions of other people, we should be ready to make allowances. The late Canon Barry used to say that it took a Frenchman to commit a mortal sin. He was rather fond of saying not quite the ordinary thing, was Canon Barry; but you saw what he meant. With our own sins, if we are in real doubt whether they were mortal or venial, we must make a prudent judgement about them, as honest and objective as we can make it; going to Communion or not going will depend on that. But in confession, as long as the sin is mentioned, I don't know that anything is gained by telling the priest whether it was or wasn't a mortal sin; let him ask questions if he wants to.

And then, having carefully divided up our sins into venial sins, those which can be pardoned, and mortal sins, which

presumably cannot be pardoned, we proceed to tell Almighty
God that we hope, by the merits of Jesus Christ, for the
pardon of *all* our sins. Once more we are plunged in an
atmosphere of mystery. The simplest way to put it, perhaps,
is this. If you think of your sin as a personal affront offered to
a personal God, the difficulty is to see why he doesn't forgive
it at once, as soon as it is committed. After all, he tells us to
forgive our enemies; why shouldn't he forgive his?

> Here lie I, Martin Elginbrodd;
> Have mercy on my soul, Lord God,
> As I would do, gin I were God
> And thou wert Martin Elginbrodd.

If, on the other hand, you think of your sin as a breach of the
eternal order of things, an upsetting of the balance of eternal
Justice, how can God forgive that? He is himself eternal
Justice; is he not, then, false to his own nature if he agrees to
treat the act irrevocably done as if it had never happened?
You and I can forgo our right to get satisfaction out of an
enemy, because the right is something external to ourselves.
But the right God has to punish us is a part of himself; how,
without ceasing to be God, can he forgo it?

There is an easy answer we are inclined to suggest at that
point, but it's one we mustn't make. We are inclined to say,
"Surely that was the whole point of the Atonement! It was
because God could not forgive us unless we made adequate
amends for our fault that Jesus Christ came to make amends
for us. If there had been any other terms on which he could
grant us forgiveness, surely he wouldn't have had recourse to
so strange an expedient as that!" But the theologians won't
let you say that. Whenever you think you have got a really
good answer to a theological difficulty, the theologians say,
"No, that's where you're wrong." It wasn't absolutely necessary for our Lord to die; it wasn't even necessary for him to
come to earth. Almighty God could have consented, if he

had wished it, to accept the sacrifice of some less worthy victim; he could have consented, if he had wished it, to forgive us our sins without demanding that any amends should be made for them at all. But he decreed that satisfaction should be made in this way; and since it has been, it is quite certain that the forgiveness to which you and I look forward is forgiveness earned on our behalf by our Blessed Lord, when he died on the Cross. . . . But the inner nature of the divine pardon is still a mystery.

There remains the question, how you and I are to avail ourselves of this gift of pardon, freely offered. As we know, we have to be sorry for our sins. Not necessarily in the sense of feeling sorry, because our feelings are not sufficiently within our own control. Sorrow for our sins is a matter of the will, not of the affections, and what is required of us is that we should unite our wills, although it be by an act which seems to awake no echo in the sensitive part of us, with the will of God. Nor is it expected of us, that we should feel certain we shall not fall into the same sins again. We know the weakness of our natures, and often the best we can do is to throw ourselves on God's mercy with the prayer that his grace will enable us to avoid sin thenceforward. We are also bound to go to confession, if we have reason to suspect that we are in mortal sin. And here, as you know, there is a distinction to be made; the distinction between perfect and imperfect contrition. Imperfect contrition, or attrition, may be dictated to us only by the fear of God, not by the love of him; that is sufficient motive if it is accompanied by actual confession to a priest. Perfect contrition, which is dictated to us by the love of God, wins us the forgiveness of our sins there and then, as long as it is accompanied by the resolve to go to confession at the earliest possible opportunity. But it is only in rare circumstances that we are encouraged to go to Communion without sacramental confession, if we have committed a mortal sin. We cannot be certain enough, being what we are, of our own dispositions.

And, as we know, contrition must be accompanied by the desire to put things right. We must mean to make restitution, if we have defrauded people of their money or their good name; we must mean to avoid the occasions of sin, as far as the way lies clear to us. If in fact those resolves afterwards break down, we nevertheless have been in a state of grace at the time when the resolves were made. But the duty of restitution doesn't disappear, and our next confession, if it is to be valid, must be accompanied by a new resolve. We must not be, consciously and deliberately, holding something back from God.

One of the most perfectly constructed lines in English poetry is, "To err is human, to forgive, divine." How perfect is the balance of those words, how rich the sense of them! They enshrine two of the greatest mysteries which, as Christians, we are bound to accept. The doctrine, I mean, that man, being what he is, can rebel against God; and the doctrine that God, being what he is, can forgive man.

19

The Sacraments

To-day is the feast of St Peter Damian, a Doctor of the Church, who died just after the Norman Conquest. He taught that there were twelve sacraments.

I hope that makes you sit up a bit, even on a cold day. You don't need to be told that there are only seven. What has gone wrong? Why, simply that we are quarrelling over the use of terms; you can't count how many sacraments there are until you have defined what a sacrament is; and that wasn't defined, even as a matter of opinion, until the twelfth century, wasn't dogmatically defined until the Council of Trent, in the sixteenth century. If St Peter Damian regarded the coronation of a king or the dedication of a church as a sacrament, that was because he was using terms in a different way. "Sacrament", after all, is only a rather meaningless word which the Latin Fathers took over to translate the Greek word *musterion*, a mystery. All the mysteries of the Christian faith, in primitive language, are sacraments of the Christian Church. What I've got to talk to you about is the list of seven sacraments which was drawn up by the Council of Trent.

Catholic theology is very fond of drawing up lists; you had a hard time of it at school, probably, swotting up all those lists at the end of the Catechism. They are rather untidy affairs, if you come to look into them. For instance, if you look up the twelve fruits of the Holy Spirit in the Greek of the New Testament, you find that there aren't twelve, there are only nine, and three false readings. And if you look up the seven gifts of the Holy Spirit in the Hebrew of the Old Testament, you find that the gift of piety isn't there; though that is probably an oversight. There are seven sacraments all right; it would be anathema to say there aren't. But when you take them in detail, they don't all square, on obvious lines, with the definition of what a sacrament is; the theologians have to start distinguishing and explaining things. Thus, in the sacrament of matrimony, you would naturally suppose that the priest was the minister, but he isn't; you would naturally suppose that the ring was the matter, but it isn't; you would naturally suppose that the form was "I, N., take thee, N.", but it isn't. However, I'm not going into all that, because I hope it is not of immediate importance for all of you. Let's cut out the official definition of a sacrament, which leads us into all sorts of puzzles, and concentrate on a quite simple statement of what the sacraments are. Only for heaven's sake don't quote me, because when you make a quite simple statement the theologians always say you've got it wrong.

A sacrament means, either, that we perform some natural action which, instead of having natural effects, has supernatural effects in the same line of country; or, that some resolution made by human wills is supernaturally ratified, so that its effect is out of all proportion to what a mere resolution of the human will could effect. Water may be expected to cleanse, food and drink to sustain, oil to strengthen and to heal, the body. Baptism, the Holy Eucharist, Confirmation, and Extreme Unction have the same kind of effects respectively, but on the soul. The other three sacraments are not quite on the same line; their office is to ratify supernaturally an intention which is already there. The man who is being ordained priest means to be a different kind of man; ordination makes him into a different kind of man. Bride and bridegroom mean to live true to one another; the grace of matrimony helps them to live true to one another. Imperfect contrition doesn't, like perfect contrition, restore us to a state of grace by itself, but when it is accompanied by sacramental confession it does.

It's obvious that Almighty God could have arranged for our justification and our sanctification without including sacraments in the programme at all. And it is equally obvious that he hasn't. That being so, there is really no more to be said; he must know best; he must have his own superlatively excellent reasons for managing things as he does. And there is no likelihood that you and I will be able, from our very limited point of view, to find out what those reasons are. But I think we might make a shot at guessing why it is that the sacraments are a good thing. It's a little dreary, don't you think, if conferences are devoted entirely to considering what objections are urged against the Catholic point of view, and why those objections are wrong? I mean, it seems to make the whole thing so negative. Perhaps this will be best; to take three obvious objections, and to show not merely why they are wrong, but that they have got hold of precisely the wrong end of the stick; the very reasons which they urge for declaring the sacraments to be a bad thing are precisely the reasons, as far as our human guesses can be trusted at all, for declaring the sacraments to be a good thing. By an odd coincidence, I think you can arrange these three objections in a historical order; each of them in turn is connected with one of the three great historic attacks which have been made on the Church as such; which have attacked her whole attitude towards life, not just some stray piece of doctrine here and there. The medieval heretics, Albigenses or Cathari or whatever you like to call them, objected to the sacramental system as being *materialistic.* The reformers of the sixteenth century objected to the sacramental system as being *magical.* The Jansenists of the seventeenth century objected to the sacramental system, or rather to certain aspects of it, as being *demoralizing.* And I think if we take those three objections in turn we shall find that the sacramental system is gain, not loss; as giving us, not the wrong view, but the right view, of matter; as saving us from certain magical notions about religion which we might otherwise be tempted to adopt; as demoralizing only in the sense that it takes religion out of the sphere of mere morality, and gives it a spiritual value instead.

The medieval heretics, whom the Dominican order was specially designed to combat, were in all probability a survival of the quite early heresy known as Manicheism. Manicheism in its turn probably came from the East; it had the Eastern vice of confusing two distinctions; the distinction between matter and spirit, and the distinction between good and evil. All matter, for the Manichee, is something bad; not created by Almighty God but by a Satanic influence which interfered with his creation. Man's soul is a prisoner in his body, not a guest. According to the medieval heretics marriage was wrong, just as wrong as concubinage; they (or at any rate the fully fledged ones) weren't allowed to take any form of animal life, or to eat any animal food, not so much as a lightly boiled egg (as the landlady said). And naturally they were all out against the sacramental system, because it tended to dignify matter and sanctify matter, which was in their view an evil thing invented by the devil.

Well, I think we've all got a little of the Manichean in us. You see it in certain modern movements; for instance, in the people who are bores about cremation. I don't mean the people who just think it is the tidiest way of doing things, but the people who seem to have a grouse against our material bodies and want to burn them as if they were a kind of refuse. And again, the extreme temperance people; not just the people who think drunkenness is a bad habit, which it is, but the people who talk about alcohol (they always call it alcohol) as if it were something essentially contaminated which has no function in life, not even in medicine. And of course the man in Samuel Butler's "Oh God, Oh Montreal" poem was another of the same lot. We've all got streaks of the thing in us; and perhaps we Catholics, who have been brought up to hear such a lot said in praise of virginity, ought to be specially on our guard against thinking of marriage as a sort of untidy second best, instead of what it is, a splendid vocation and a high sacrament. In order to see life straight and to meet life square, you have to be continually resisting temptations that are connected with sex and yet never for a moment tell yourself that sex is a bad thing; that it is something which, even in marriage, tends to drag you down. That's a terribly dangerous frame of mind to get into, in marriage or out of it. Matter is a part of our world, and a part of our nature; Almighty God has paid us the compliment, which he never paid to the holy angels, of making us a kind of liaison officers between matter and spirit; we've got to accept the things of sense, and to hallow them. To make that difficult job easier for us, he himself took flesh at the Incarnation; and then, by way of continuing the mystery of his Incarnation for all time, gave us the sacraments to link the life of the flesh with the life of the spirit. That first, then; from the moment when water is poured over us at the font to the moment when oil is smeared over us on our death-beds, we have got to welcome God's material creatures as expressions of his goodness, renewed by our Redemption.

Now, I think there probably was a certain connexion between the medieval heretics and the authors of the Reformation, fascinating but far too long to go into. In any case, the Reformation attack on the sacraments came from a different angle. The Reformers didn't object to sacramental doctrine as something materialistic. *They* didn't condemn marriage; quite the contrary, they were all for it. No, but their idea was that the human soul ought to approach God only by faith in Jesus Christ; sacraments might be useful as mere symbols, as helping to stimulate that faith; but the idea of a priest coming between the worshipper and his God, or of outward ceremonies actually having the power to advance our salvation, was just so much magic. Of course, logically they hadn't a leg to stand on over infant Baptism; the Baptists and the Quakers have always been the really logical Protestants. But that was the essence of their protest.

I need hardly say that it is extremely common nowadays, outside the Church, to condemn the sacramental system on the ground that it is magical, as Bishop Barnes, of Birmingham, does. I expect you know the story of his meeting a Catholic priest on a railway platform. The priest recognized Bishop Barnes, but he didn't give himself away when they got talking; and at the end, when the Bishop asked, "May I know who it is I've had the pleasure of meeting?" he said, "Oh, I'm the local magician." After all, one says to oneself, what is the exact difference between a witch-doctor who whisks you with an elephant's tail to cure you of sunstroke, and a man dressed up in a mitre who gives you a slap on the cheek and tells you to receive the Holy Ghost? Isn't the technique rather the same?

I hope I'm not being perverse about it, but it always seems to me that the sacramental process, instead of being just the same as magic, is the precise opposite of magic. Magic, surely, means using supernatural means—or so they are regarded— to produce a natural effect; to cure an illness, to get the wireworm out of the mealie-crop, something of that kind. Whereas the sacramental process is using natural means to produce supernatural effects. The blow on the cheek and the smudge of oil on the forehead are expected to fortify the soul with a higher measure of the Holy Spirit's influence; surely we ought to call that ceremony by some name which is the exact opposite of magic? I quite admit that some of the minor ceremonies in baptism, the insufflation, for example, come nearer the mark; but then, these are relics of exorcism, they are not part of the baptism proper. I quite admit that extreme unction would be a more questionable ceremony to defend, if we regarded it chiefly as a means of making the sick person well; but we don't—on the contrary, the Church is very loth to let us have it unless she feels quite certain we can't get well. The removal of the last stains of our sins, that is what the ritual talks about, all the time when the unctions are taking place; it is only in the prayers at the end, which generally don't get said, that we hear anything about the sick person's health. After all, in a primitive society the medicine man is not the forerunner of the priest, he is the forerunner of the scientist. The function of science has been defined— by me, I think—as discovering the causes of things, and escaping their consequences. And that is what the magician was up to; he was doing his best to checkmate nature, only (as the result of inadequate observation and experiment) he was going the wrong way about it. He tried the elephant's tail, in the hope that it might do some good, because the Jesuits hadn't yet discovered quinine.

No, if people tell you that our sacraments have points of affinity with the old mystery religions, I think you have to admit that that is true as far as it goes. Only, we don't think of the sacraments as having been invented by the Church in an effort to cut out the mystery religions; we claim that the mystery religions, in so far as they were really primitive, were God's way of preparing the world for the Christian sacra- ments. But it's no use talking about magic; not for Protes- tants, anyhow. Curiously enough, I think the boot is on the other leg; I think Protestantism, where it has been at its most characteristic, has run much truer to the magical formula. Because, as we said, the magician hopes to produce natural effects by supernatural means; and in very much the same way the Protestant expects to have interior consolations as part of his religion, floods of tears, transports of joy, such as the early Wesleyans were always going in for; anyhow, a com- fortable feeling inside. And there, once again, I think the sacramental system gives us Catholics an advantage. We don't expect to *feel* much as the result of the grace which, we know, we are getting. We are accustomed to the idea of supernatural transactions going on; affecting quite really the state of our souls; and yet nothing in the way of external feelings to show for it. We are content to go on in faith, knowing that we have received spiritual benefits without having the itch to take our spiritual temperatures all the time.

And that brings me on to my last point, the Jansenist protest. The Jansenists as a whole never went into schism; they remained for more than a century a dissatisfied body within the Church. Their doctrinal errors about grace don't concern us here. But, side by side with those errors, and in an odd way rather inconsistently with those errors, the Jansenists quarrelled with the free-and-easy way in which (under Jesuit influence, *they* said) Catholics treated the sacraments. They thought that confessors were far too easy with our sins, and that people were encouraged to go to Communion much more frequently than their spiritual state warranted. They boasted of pious Jansenists who had stayed away from Communion for months, or for years occasionally, out of reverence for our Lord's Body and Blood. You will see for yourselves that there was something in that protest; it is one which needs to be made from time to time, only the Jansenists were pedantic and contumacious about it.

They thought that the sacramental system, unless the discipline of it were tightened up, was *demoralizing*. And so it can be, of course, if you and I get inclined to take things too easily. Unless chaplains have changed a great deal in the last ten years, you don't need to hear anything from me about that. But meanwhile, as I was saying, I think the sacramental system helps to keep in our view something which can never be kept too clearly in our view, the fact of our complete dependence on Divine grace. A person who tries to live a life that's pleasing to God without any sacraments to help him is always in danger of measuring everything by his own effort, and becoming rather smug and priggish about his own effort. But the sacramental system, whatever else it does, ought to teach us humility. Almighty God himself shows amazing condescension in using material things as the vehicles of his grace; in the holy Sacrament of the Altar you can almost say that he turns himself into the instrumental cause of our

sanctification. And on our side, we approach the sacraments
with humility; how else could we approach them? When you
were a kid at school, in shorts, a bishop came and confirmed
you. Probably you will tell me that the show you have put up
since isn't a great advertisement for the sacramental system;
you haven't been a particularly strong Christian. No, but you
would have been a weaker Christian without that ceremony.
And the difference wasn't of your making; it was something
God did for you and in you. That's true of grace generally,
but it is most obviously, most self-evidently true of sacramental grace, simply because the means used to secure it are so
inadequate, viewed in themselves, to the effect they produce.
Who are you and I to dwell with satisfaction on our own
efforts? Why, we are the servants of a God who turns an
infant child from a heathen into a Christian with a drop of
water!

To get matter and spirit in their right perspective, to serve
God without hankering after interior consolations, to keep
in mind our utter dependence on him, all *that* comes easier
to those who live by a sacramental system.

20

The Priesthood

Let us begin our conference about the priesthood with a little dissertation on language. There is a word in Greek which means a sacrificial agent, *hiereus*. And there is a word in Latin which means a sacrificial agent, *sacerdos*. Read all through the New Testament in Greek, and you will never find the word *hiereus* used of a Christian minister. Read all through the New Testament in Latin, and you will never find the word *sacerdos* used of a Christian minister. Read through the Douay version, and you *will* find the word "priest" so used, in one or two passages; but not in the new American revision, nor in Knox. The word here is not *hiereus*, but *presbuteros*, and it is less confusing, though rather ugly, if we transliterate that word, instead of translating it, and call it "presbyter". The first Christians, you see, made a distinction. When they were talking about a man set apart for the worship of Jupiter, they called him a sacrificial agent. When they were talking about a man set apart for the service of Almighty God under the old, Jewish covenant, they called him a sacrificial agent. But when they were talking about a man set apart for the service of Almighty God under the new covenant, they called him a *presbuteros*, an elder. Not meaning that he was necessarily an old man with a white beard, any more than a "senior" member of the Common Room is necessarily an old man with a white beard. The point about a *presbuteros* is exactly the same as the point about a senior member of Common Room; he is a foundation member, he belongs to the establishment.

In arguing, never disguise from yourself the strength of the
other man's case. The Reformers, when they claimed that
there was no warrant in Scripture for regarding the Christian
ministry as a sacrificial priesthood, were choosing quite a
good wicket to play on. The word *hiereus* is used, in the New
Testament, of our Blessed Lord, in a mystical sense; it is also
used of Christian people generally in a mystical sense; "you
are a royal priesthood". Isn't it obvious, said the Reformers,
that in the Christian Church the idea of sacrificial priesthood
survives only as a metaphor? That the people whom the
Apostles left to carry on their work were simply pastors, who
preached the gospel and looked after men's souls? You could
call them *presbuteroi*, elders, to express their dignity, or you
could call them *episcopoi*, overseers, to denote their office—
but you didn't call them *hiereis*, sacrificial agents, as you would
have if you had regarded the Lord's Supper, in the first century of the Christian era, as a sacrificial act. Well, you know,
if the New Testament records had referred to a sect which
died out about A.D. 70, so that it had no subsequent history
by which we could check it, I think that is, very likely, the
picture we should have formed for ourselves. If you take the
Bible only, uncorrected by the findings of tradition, as your
rule of faith, it is uncommonly hard to prove that the first-
century presbyter thought of himself as what we mean by
a priest, or that the first-century *episcopos* thought of himself
as what we mean by a bishop. It's far easier to prove the
doctrine of the Papacy from the New Testament, than the
doctrine of episcopacy.

Only, you see, the Christian religion didn't come to an
end in A.D. 70; it lasted on, and has preserved a living tradition, which would be there all the same, even if the books of
the New Testament had never been written. It is true, things
don't stand still; there is a tendency for institutions to develop, and it could be argued that the Christian religion
started as a kind of Nonconformist affair and developed, later
on, into a Catholic Church with a fully fledged hierarchy. I

need hardly say that people have supported that view with great violence, especially during the nineteenth century, when everybody was mad about evolution and it looked a mere child's play for anything to develop into anything else. But you've got to show when it was that the development took place, and what protest was made against it at the time, or alternatively why the protest wasn't made. The favourite supposition used to be that the Church went all Catholic about the middle of the second century. But, most unfortunately, there was a schism in the middle of the second century which would quite certainly have made capital out of it if the Church, at that very moment, had been declining from the simplicity of her primitive ideals. I mean the Montanist schism, which is amply documented for us by the writings of a really brilliant heretic, Tertullian. And there is no suggestion to be found in the writings of Tertullian that there had been any funny business going on. The more carefully people study our Christian records, the further they find themselves driven back in the attempt to fix the date when the Church started going wrong. And I think very few scholars would now deny that the picture you get in the Apocalypse of Almighty God sitting on a throne with an altar in front of him, surrounded by twenty-four elders, is simply based on a piece of primitive liturgy; the bishop at his throne in front of the altar with his presbyters standing round him. Which is not a Nonconformist picture in the least.

At this point you are probably wanting to ask, "Why, then, in heaven's name, was the early Church so careful to avoid the word, *hiereus*, *sacerdos*, sacrificial agent, if the early Church felt exactly the same about the Mass as we do?" The answer to that one, I think, is quite simple. By a kind of unconscious instinct, human language shrinks from ambiguity. And the first Christians will have avoided the word *hiereus*, without asking themselves why they did it, simply because it was the ordinary word for a priest attached to the Temple at Jerusalem, and it would have been confusing to apply it, all of a sudden, to a quite different class of people. A curious verse early on in the Acts of the Apostles tells us that a large number of priests had given their allegiance to the faith. What became of them? Did they go on functioning as temple priests? We don't know. There is no evidence that they stopped. In any case, what we tend to forget about the very early Church is that it existed side by side with the synagogue, and, in Jerusalem at any rate, at very close quarters. And if a presbyter of that period had taken to calling himself a priest, it would have been just as confusing as if a Catholic priest in modern England took to describing himself as a parson. We have just as much right to be called parsons as the Anglicans have. But we shouldn't do it, because it would be confusing. So they didn't call themselves *hiereis*; but they did not thereby mean to suggest that they were not sacrificial agents. After all, a priest has a lot of other things to do, even nowadays, besides saying Mass. He has got to administer all the other sacraments, and to preach the word of God, and to make his books balance. So they called themselves presbyters, senior members of the Church. And that is still, it is well to remind ourselves, the official title of a Catholic priest. He calls himself *sacerdos* by a kind of graceful analogy; but his official title is *presbyter*.

But of course the reason why the old-fashioned kind of Protestant dislikes the idea of a priesthood isn't a mere matter of antiquarian prejudice. He may complain that he "can't find it in the Bible"; but his reason isn't that he can't find it in the Bible. His reason is, as he will tell you himself, that he "doesn't like the idea of a fellow man coming between him and his God". And that, I think, gives us a convenient point of departure for studying the sacramental character of the priesthood. At the root of it, that kind of criticism is a criticism of the sacramental system altogether. Obviously, if he had seen fit to do it, Almighty God could have enabled us to reach our supernatural end without the use of sacraments at all. We all know that a spiritual Communion, faithfully made,

produces all the effects of sacramental Communion; God
might have decreed that no Communions should be made at
all except spiritual ones. We all know that an act of perfect
contrition wins us, then and there, absolution of our sins
before we ever go into the confessional; God might have
dispensed with the confessional, and accepted our act of imperfect contrition instead. And there is, perhaps, a kind of
mystical temper, inside the Church and still more outside it,
to which the whole sacramental approach means comparatively little; it will frequent the sacraments out of obedience,
but they do not appeal to its imagination. That was not God's
will for most of us. His will was that as we were composite
creatures, mind and matter at once, matter should have its
part in perfecting the work of our redemption; water and
bread and wine and oil should be endowed with a supernatural efficacy which would overflow from the body into the
soul. And if you are going to have sacraments, you will want
human ministers to dispense the sacraments. Why exactly
should that be so?

We all know that there is one sacrament of which no priest
and no bishop in the Western rite, not even the Holy Father
himself, can be the minister; the sacrament of matrimony.
The bride and the bridegroom minister that sacrament to
one another. You can't minister a sacrament to yourself; there
was a queer character called John Smith, early in the seventeenth century, who baptized himself and has gone down to
history as John Smith the Sebaptist; but I understand it didn't
really count. Still, lay people can baptize, as we know; why
shouldn't they celebrate the other sacraments as well? Why
should there be people specially set apart for it?

The answer to that is surely that the priest himself is a kind
of sacrament, a sacrament of fatherhood. The sacramental
system, as we know, develops the supernatural on the lines of
the natural; water washes us, oil strengthens us, bread feeds
us, wine cheers us, in the supernatural as in the natural order.
And in the natural order no man lives and no man dies to

himself; each of us exists first and foremost as a member of a family. If you hadn't a father, you wouldn't have been here at all. And the sacramental system is based on the idea of the family; each parish is a family, and its father is the parish priest. The priest at the font is the father bringing children to life, supernatural life. The priest at the altar is the father as bread-winner, giving the supernatural family, as it gathers round a common table, its supernatural food. The priest in the confessional is the father exercising discipline within the family, correcting and training up his children. That is why the Church, in her wisdom, has not left the vow of celibacy to the monks; she enjoins it on the secular clergy as well. But for a different reason; the monk goes into his cloister so as to get away from the distractions and from the consolations of family life. The secular priest remains single because he already has a family to provide for, his parish. A single life, said Bacon, doeth well with churchmen, for charity will scarce cover the ground, when it must first fill a pool. And all the Catholics within the boundaries of the parish, including the lags in gaol and the lunatics in the asylums, are the priest's children. That is why the rector of a parish is under a strict obligation to say Mass for his parishioners every Sunday and every holyday. He is like Job, offering sacrifice for his sons and daughters; "Who knows, thought he, but they may have committed some fault, these children of mine?" That is why many of you are confusing, really, the whole Catholic idea, when you go off to Mass at the Cathedral or the Oratory, and don't know the way to your parish church. You are breaking up the supernatural family.

Fathers are not always very discerning, and when I give a meditation to priests, I point out that a priest ought to be the mother of his parish as well as the father of it, which is quite a different thing. That makes them sit up rather, but it's all in St Paul. However, I won't talk about that this morning, because it wouldn't be good for you; it's a scolding for priests only.

Anyhow, don't get worried when Protestants of the old-fashioned sort tell you that the priest comes between you and your God. Like so many of these cant phrases, it depends on a very simple ambiguity of language. There are things which come between you and your destination by preventing you from getting there, like a barbed-wire fence. And there are things which come between you and your destination in the sense of helping you to get there, like a bridge over a river. And the institution of the priesthood is something which makes it easier for you to get to God by way of that sacramental approach which he has given us for a comfort. The institution of the priesthood rounds off the sacramental system by making it clear to us that it is a family system; the priest is the father of the family and the head of the family, and when we gather at certain points of contact, the font which is our family washing-place, and the altar which is our family table, and the confessional which is our family stool of repentance, it is by his means that we avail ourselves of those mercies which God grants to us as a family. You may have two bridges side by side, a road-bridge to carry heavy traffic and a foot-bridge a bit further along. Nobody grudges you the foot-bridge of private prayer, of meditation, of contemplation, by which you can reach God as a lonely unit, not bothering for the time being about priesthood or sacraments. But when we all come before God as a single united family, the priesthood is the great wide road-bridge by which we do it.

We haven't yet quite told the whole truth, have we, about the priesthood. Because there is one contact of our daily Christian life in which the priest becomes something more than the father who leads and feeds us and fends for us. I mean the actual celebration of the Holy Mass, in which the priest becomes our representative before God, and even in some sense God's representative to us. The priest when he puts on the sacred vestments puts on, liturgically, the person of Christ. Our Lord in the sacrifice of the holy Mass is both priest and victim; as victim, he is represented to us by the thing which lies on the altar, as priest he is represented to us by the man who stands at the altar. It is to the priest that we commit our intentions, as if to make sure that they will become part of the stuff of his sacrifice; it is from the priest that we receive those salutations and benedictions which radiate outwards from the altar to us and to all faithful people. Inevitably, during those moments of his commerce with the unseen, the priest becomes to us a living symbol of our own corporate emotion. He is our father, now, in a mystical and inclusive capacity, like Aaron with the twelve stones in his breastplate commemorating the twelve tribes of Israel. But all this is transient; this, his most sacred character, is something the priest puts on and takes off with the vestments he wears. Just as the judge, on leaving the bench, is no longer the representative of government but a private citizen, so the priest, back in the sacristy, has his feet on earth once more.

How much exactly does he come back to earth? That is, I suppose, the chief difficulty and the chief danger of a priest's life; how much can he ever afford to be off duty? When I was teaching at St Edmund's, the boys who came round for confession used to finish up with the invariable formula, "Thank you very much, Father. Good-night, Sir." You had become a master again. What I've been trying to suggest in this conference is that this engaging schoolboy attitude doesn't do full justice to the idea of the priesthood. I've left a lot of things out; I've said nothing about the priesthood in relation to the rest of the hierarchy—bishops, for example; is a bishop a kind of glorified priest? Or ought we to think of a priest as a bishop with his wings clipped? And I've said nothing about the other orders which lead up to the priesthood, or the fascinating speculations of theologians about whether an acolyte has four rings round his head or only one, when he goes to heaven or alternatively to hell. I've simply concentrated on what seems to me to be the essential point about the priesthood, in relation to the laity at any rate. A priest isn't to be thought of as a mere sacrificial beast of burden; as an umbrella-stand to hang your Mass intentions on, or an automatic machine where you put your rosary in and it comes out blessed. He is an integral part of that parish-family which is the cell of Christendom; indeed, he is the pivotal man, the lynch-pin of it. *Hanc igitur oblationem servitutis nostrae, sed et cunctae familiae tuae. . . . Nos servi tui, sed et plebs tua sancta*—the functions and the destinies of clergy and laity are interlocked; and in that sense, if our critics complain that the priest comes between a man and his God, we shall not be concerned to deny it.

21

The Christian Notion of Marriage

If you should come across the works of the great theologian Suarez, in the latest and most elaborate edition, turn to the Index volume and look up the word *mulier* (which is the Latin for "woman"). The entry you will find in the index is a very simple one; it runs: "Mulier, vide Scandalum". There are a great many people who imagine that this phrase sums up the attitude of the Catholic Church towards sex. There are a lot of references which you could dig up if you took the trouble, especially from the more desert sort of Fathers, which are calculated to bear out that impression; the Fathers of the Church will have their little grouse now and again. What is worse (because we are not talking controversy now, we are trying to get our own ideas properly cleared up), we ourselves are apt to think at the back of our minds as if sex were something of which the Church disapproves, something consequently which must be rather wrong. Marriage, yes, she allows marriage; but is it after all perhaps only as a *faute de mieux*? Is it by a kind of reluctant dispensation that she gives the faithful a let-up from their normal duty of life-long virginity, because if she didn't the faithful would go on strike, and incidentally there would be no baptisms? That would explain, perhaps, why she makes marriage so difficult, all those legal formalities, all those heavy fees, and the understanding that if you do contract marriage you have got to have an uncomfortably large family, and whatever happens you can never, never get out of it?

That is the idea which flits about at the back of our minds, in our more jaundiced moments, masquerading as the Christian notion of marriage. And of course it is all wrong from beginning to end. For Christians, marriage is a sacrament; and you may almost say that for Christians it is *the* sacrament *par excellence*. Not in the sense that it is the most important on the list, obviously. No, but in the sense that it helps us, more than any of the others, to understand what the word "sacrament" means. Quite true, it is a sacrament with a difference; the matter of it is not what we ordinarily mean by matter, the form of it is nowhere laid down as of necessity, and the ministers of it are not at all the people you expect them to be. All that is true, but there's this to be said on the other side; matrimony is the only sacrament which is *called* a sacrament in the Bible. A man will leave his father and mother, St Paul says to the Ephesians, and will cling to his wife, and the two will become one flesh. Yes, those words are a high mystery—*sacramentum*, of course, is just a token-word used to represent the Greek *musterion*. Those words, you see, go right back behind the Christian dispensation, go right back to the creation of man and woman, and yet they are sacramental. That is as much as to say that marriage is a *natural* sacrament; although it could not confer grace until the reign of grace had begun, it had all the characteristics of a sacramental transaction. Because, define the word "sacrament" how you will, the root idea of it is clearly this, that something purely spiritual and something purely physical are presented close side by side. And in human marriage, even when it involves no shred of religious observance, that dual character hits you in the face. Love, which is the most spiritual thing given in our experience outside of religion, is there side by side with the satisfaction of a purely physical desire; the angel in us and the animal in us are both at work, and not as contrasts or opposites. Spiritual aspiration finds its expression in, and is fostered by, the brute facts of biology.

I said we weren't going to talk controversy, but it's well to get that point clearly in our minds, because it makes it easier to understand one of the puzzles you'll probably hear discussed one of these Sundays: I mean, that the Church recognizes a marriage between two non-Catholics as valid, even if it's two unbaptized gypsies marrying over the tongs. More and more, we Catholics are getting driven into a corner in which we think of divorce and remarriage as something which is quite right and natural for everybody except ourselves. But of course it isn't; and when our friends say, in a half-admiring, half-pitying tone, "Of course you Catholics aren't allowed to get divorced and remarried", your real job is to answer, "You mean, we Catholics *know it's wrong* to get divorced and remarried." Monogamy is not a Catholic stunt; it's God's law for the human race. I don't say it's easy to get people to see that, because of course the animals don't set us a very good example—except swans, I think we're told that the same pair of swans mate year after year: but it seems to make them very ill-tempered, especially in early summer. Well, of course, there are all sorts of reasons why the behaviour of the other animals doesn't concern us. It's not such a long-term job for them looking after a family, when their children grow up in a few months, whereas ours don't grow up properly for sixteen or seventeen years. We, unlike the animals, can connect past impressions by memory; we, unlike the animals, can meet future events by foresight. But most of all, we human beings differ from the animals in our capacity for idealizing and sublimating the relations of the sexes; we can transmute passion into romance. And therefore man and woman who solemnly agree to share the rest of their lives are celebrating a kind of *natural* sacrament, even if they do it without invoking any kind of religious sanction, or holding any kind of religious belief. Their experience has transcended the limits of the bodily and the temporal, pushed through into the domain of spirit, where all is eternal.

But matrimony under the Christian dispensation becomes

something infinitely more exciting. You may almost say that matrimony, rather than baptism, is the gate of the sacraments. Baptism, after all, derives its efficacy from the Incarnation, from the act by which our Lord incorporates us into himself; the Mystical Body is the matrix of our spiritual rebirth. And the Church is the Bride of Christ, the wedding comes before the christening. But, you say, that is only a metaphor. You know, I think St Paul would have hated to hear you talk like that. Immediately after the words I quoted just now, about the great mystery, he goes on to the real point: "Those words are a great mystery, and I am applying them to Christ and his Church." And in the same passage, "the man is the head to which the woman is united, just as Christ is the head of the Church." St Paul is always talking like that; in the Corinthians he makes it even more explicit: "The head to which a wife is united is her husband, just as the head to which every man is united is Christ; so too, the head to which Christ is united is God." I don't pretend that St Paul is using very feminist language. You have to make allowance, I think, for the times in which he lived; you must remember the sort of position married women occupied in his day, remember the old Roman's epitaph on his wife, which runs, DOMI MANSIT LANAM FECIT VALE—"She stayed at home and got on with her knitting; good-bye." But, leaving all that controversial matter on one side, the point of what St Paul is saying is that the bond which unites man and wife is the same bond which unites Christ and his Church; and therefore in a sense is the same bond which unites Manhood and Divinity in Christ himself. Marriage, Christian marriage, is the analogue and the extension of the Incarnation.

New Testament theology, you see, has that fearless mystical approach which always interprets the lower in terms of the higher; spirit, not matter, is the *reality*—you get it especially in our Lord's discourses in St John. And you get it in St Paul; he refers to Almighty God as the Father from whom all fatherhood in heaven and earth is named; you see what that means? We talk as if Mr Jones was a father in the literal sense, and Almighty God could only be called the Father by a metaphor; no, says St Paul, it's Almighty God who is literally a father; it's a kind of metaphor when we use the word "father" in relation to Mr Jones. And so here; he doesn't say that human marriage is a convenient illustration by which we can make it more clear to ourselves what the Incarnation means. No, we shan't begin to understand human marriage until we realize that it is a kind of image of the Incarnation, an echo of the Incarnation. Contemplate the love of Christ for his Church, and then you may form some idea of what love between a Christian man and a Christian woman really means. For it is as an extension of the Divine love that human love exists.

"Well," you say, "that all sounds very fine, but it's a bit like what they fed to us in the sermon when my sister got married last vac. And of course it went down all right at the time, naturally, when they were all keyed up about one another, and just off on the honeymoon. But does that kind of thing last? My sister is quite a good sort, and so's the man she married, but I should think in about five years from now they'll have started jogging along much like other people, making a success of their marriage and all that, don't you know, but not wanting all that appeal to the higher emotions. Surely the Church would be better, on such occasions, to give the bride and bridegroom a straight, practical talk about the difficulties and dangers of married life? Because after all that's what they will be up against before long."

I'm very glad you raised that point. Because the underlying suggestion of it seems to me so exactly the opposite of the truth. The suggestion, I mean, that the Church is sentimental about weddings, and the world is realistic about them. Surely it is just the other way round? It is the world, not the Church, which gets intoxicated with the smell of the orange-blossom, and imagines that love simply means two people feeling gooey about each other. And that is what makes all the trouble, that's what is filling the divorce-courts. (Notice how naturally I pronounce that word differently from you. I call it DIvorce, you call it DIVVorce. That's because I think of it as a strange, exotic Latin word, like divert and divest, whereas you think it's an ordinary English word like divine. So far we have travelled in fifty years.) Of course if by "love" you mean the sensation of three weeks on the Riviera, that is not going to last, and the only way to satisfy your ambitions is to make your life into a round of honeymoons. But the Church, with her doctrine that marriage is a sacrament, is much more realistic. She says, "Oh, you want to get married, do you? That means, you want to imitate the action of Jesus Christ in his Incarnation. Well, God bless you; you will want all the grace I can rout out for you if you are to do that—a whole trousseau of graces." She thinks at once, not of the fun you are going to have, but of the qualities you will need.

It is, of course, a permanent mystery why God ever created anything. As the theologians point out, the existence of something other than himself could not increase either his essential glory or his happiness. The only account of it they can offer is to say that goodness is *diffusivum sui*, goodness is always looking for a reservoir into which it can overflow. And something of the same difficulty arises if we ask ourselves the question, Why did our Lord come to redeem us? St John has put it once for all in the phrase, "God showed his love for us first", and St Paul in the phrase, "while we were yet sinners, Christ died for us." God showed his love for us; it is the aorist, not the present; "God loved us" will not do. I hadn't the courage to put in my translation what I wanted to put, "God fell in love with us." And yet, if we want to bring the doctrine of the Incarnation home to our minds, I'm not sure it isn't the right way of putting it; our Lord Jesus Christ fell in love with us, and while we were still sinners. How *could* he do that? Well, I suppose there is one quite simple answer you can give; he loved us not for what we were, but for what he saw he was going to make of us. He found us wallowing in the mire, and he saw in us that spotless Bride we were one day to be. Dare we say, he idealized us? . . . Anyhow, the point which is important for us at the moment is that if our Lord did that, his love for us was wholly unselfish. It was all *giving*; there was nothing he could get out of us, except what was already his gift. In this great Romance which is the archetype, and is meant to be the inspiration, of all Christian marriage, the operative force was utter unselfishness.

I don't mean you to conclude that in human marriage either side ought to be trying, consciously, to correct the faults of the other; that is a very dangerous experiment. I don't even mean to say that either side ought deliberately to idealize the other; though in a half-conscious way a good deal of that goes on in some marriages; women are much better at it than men. "Be to her faults a little blind"—it was a cynical poet who wrote it, but I don't think the advice was altogether cynical. No, what we have to imitate about our Lord's love for his Church is its unselfishness. In the early days of a romance, there is no difficulty about that; it comes natural to us to be unselfish. But it will, by almost imperceptible degrees, become more of an effort to play up to him or her, to make allowances. And the chief end for which we ought to ask God's grace, when we marry, is that exactly in proportion as romance fades, and unselfishness becomes more of an effort, less spontaneous, Divine grace should step in and keep us at it just the same. If you will have the common sense to make that prayer, and to mean it, then I think the process by which calculated unselfishness comes into play will be as imperceptible as the process by which spontaneous unselfishness fades out; neither side will be conscious of taking the strain—and that is eminently desirable. Unless, of course, you marry someone quite unsuitable, or circumstances make your married life a difficult one. In that case, you will certainly feel the effort; please God, you will make it.

When I talk about unselfishness, I don't just mean helping to wash up. Washing up is a very important thing nowadays, and I think it can be an excellent symbol of unselfishness. But the whole thing, of course, goes much deeper than that; a successful marriage means that two people are successfully conspiring to live a shared life. Although, as I say, I think it's a dangerous experiment for either party to set about influencing the other, both parties are as a matter of fact influencing each other the whole time. Part of God's design for the sanctification of your soul is the influence which husband or wife is going to have on you. When I was here as chaplain, and only looked after the men, I used to say I hoped they would all marry admirable Catholic wives, because I didn't see any other hope of their salvation. And I've no doubt that if I were in Mgr Elwes' place I should be saying exactly the same about the women. After all, there is not all that difference between marrying and entering religion. The man or woman who enters religion does so with a twofold object; to achieve his or her own sanctification in and through the community, and to help the other members of it to achieve theirs. That object will not be attained, unless he or she brings to the task an unselfishness which is prepared to live in and with and for the life of the community. There must be a certain abridgement of one's own personality if community life, or married life, is to be a success. But the abridgement of your life will, commonly at least, be the enrichment of your character.

Which reminds me that one aspect of life in a religious community is the admission of postulants. I wonder if any Catholic sermon on marriage has ever gone on so long without mentioning children? But it was done on purpose; I wanted to put before you the essential characteristics of Christian marriage, and we mustn't forget that if it is God's will a childless marriage can nevertheless be completely sanctified. What you ought to be clear about at present is that marriage, even taken by itself, is a vocation. It is part of that structure of destiny which God has designed for you; he has called you to serve him in this particular way, to be intimately responsible for the happiness, in time and in eternity, of a life other than your own.

22

Our Lord's Teaching on Marriage and Divorce

I can't imagine anything more boring than the conference I am just about to give you. I shall deal entirely with a single utterance of our Lord's, perhaps made on two occasions, perhaps only on one occasion. It is concerned with the question, on which heaven knows we want a plain answer, whether a valid marriage can ever be dissolved, in such a way that either party is free to remarry, while the other partner is still alive. And, it is just our luck, the Evangelists don't tell the same story; or don't appear to. Put off their stroke by this appearance of disharmony, the copyists who were responsible for producing our present manuscripts lose their heads, and start giving us different readings in their turn. The facts cannot be accurately conveyed except to those who have rather a precise knowledge of Greek, and a workmanlike knowledge of Hebrew. Quite honestly, I pity you. I can only do my best to make the whole thing clear; no treatment in the world could make it lively.

Probably—you can't be certain—our Lord made a public utterance on this subject at least twice. The first occasion was in the course of his ordinary teaching; perhaps a whole crowd of people were there, perhaps only the disciples. For some reason, we don't know why, he touched on the subject of divorce; perhaps, as so often, he was insisting that it wasn't safe to follow the moral teaching of the Pharisees, it was too lax. Anyhow, he made it clear that for two married people to separate, just because they didn't get on, and choose fresh partners, was simply adultery. That is recorded for us in the fifth chapter of St Matthew, and in the sixteenth chapter of St Luke. The saying has probably come adrift from its original context, in both gospels; in St Matthew it *looks* as if it came into the argument of the Sermon on the Mount, but read through the chapter again, leaving out verses 31 and 32, and I think you will find that the unity of the context really gains by the omission. But because we don't know *when* our Lord said a thing, we mustn't conclude that he didn't say it.

Then I think the Pharisees heard about it; I imagine the Pharisees did hear about most of the things our Lord said. And they thought it would be a good opportunity for making him say something unpopular. There were two schools of thought among themselves about divorce; some of them thought it ought only to be allowed with very grave reason, others thought it ought to be made pretty easy. So it was quite simple to ask him about it, as if they were submitting their differences to arbitration; and anything he said could probably be used in evidence against him. They asked him, "Is it right for a man to put away his wife, for whatever cause?" Being English, we read that phrase (I made it ambiguous on purpose) as meaning "even for a slight cause". Being Jews, they probably meant "even for a grave cause"; but it doesn't matter much. Then he told them about the divine institution of marriage, and how Moses had permitted divorce "to suit their hard hearts". And he added a condemnation of divorce in almost the same terms, if not exactly the same terms, which he had used on the previous occasion. This incident is recorded by St Matthew in chapter xix, and by St Mark in chapter x.

So far, so good. But this is where the trouble starts. If we had only St Mark and St Luke to go upon, our Lord, on both occasions, forbade the remarriage of divorced persons, and forbade it absolutely. "If a man puts away his wife and marries another, he behaves adulterously towards her; and if a woman puts away her husband and marries another, she is an adulteress." That is St Mark, and St Luke's account is practically the same, except that he puts the blame in the second half of the sentence on the corespondent, not on the respondent. But St Matthew, in both passages, upsets the whole apple-cart. According to him, what our Lord said on the first occasion was, "The man who puts away his wife (setting aside the matter of unfaithfulness) makes an adulteress of her." And what our Lord said on the second occasion was, "He who puts away his wife, not for any unfaithfulness of hers, and so marries another, commits adultery." In the remaining part of the sentence, he agrees with St Luke and he agrees with St Mark, but by that time the harm has been done. Surely in either case the saving clause implies that you *can* put away the unfaithful wife and marry another woman instead, without being, in our Lord's view, an adulterer?

Now, if we were Protestants, and believed what nearly all Protestants do about the relative value of the different gospels, and their dependence on one another, the whole thing would be plain sailing. It's a curious thing, but in a really tidy world we Catholics would be allowing divorce, and the Protestants would be forbidding it. We should be saying, "Well, of course St Mark and St Luke don't seem to like the idea, but St Matthew has a very useful probable opinion about it." Whereas the Protestants would reply, "Matthew? Oh, he doesn't count." You see, they *will* have it that St Matthew wrote much later than St Mark, copying down St Mark's stuff and then editing it in various ways to suit his own purposes. What St Mark says is what our Lord said, and what St Matthew says is a doctored edition of it, colored by the views of A.D. 90 or worse. If you quote to them the text about "Thou art Peter", they tell you at once, "*That* doesn't count; it's not in St Mark." So it's a very useful *argumentum ad hominem* to point out to our Protestant friends that what St Matthew says about the guilty wife doesn't count either. It isn't our Lord, it's just the pseudo-Matthew.

However, being what we are, we are committed to a different account of the matter. It is the general consensus of opinion among Catholic theologians that St Matthew wrote the first of the four gospels; he wrote it in Aramaic, and we don't know when our existing Greek version of it was made, or by whom, but the substance of it was written down by an eyewitness of our Lord's own career. And in any case, St Matthew was inspired, and he wouldn't have been inspired to give a quite imaginary account of what our Lord said, and one which tallies neither with St Mark nor with St Luke. Even if we were monks living on Mount Athos, with no women in the peninsula at all, we should still be furiously interested in these two texts of St Matthew, because somehow or another the gospels have got to be harmonized. How did our Lord manage to say something so obscure that what St Matthew says he said is quite different, at first sight, from what St Mark and St Luke say he said? For the matter of that, you can throw in St Paul. In the seventh chapter of his first epistle to the Corinthians, he attributes to our Lord the same teaching as you find in St Mark and St Luke.

It isn't surprising that some commentators, including some Catholics, regard the saving clause as a false reading; the words were never used by our Lord, never attributed to him by St Matthew or by the translator of St Matthew; they either crept into the text by error, or were foisted into the text by some unscrupulous copyist, at a very early date. In defense of that view, they point out that the text, as I have already mentioned, does show signs of disturbance at this point. In that one verse of Matthew xix there are two major differences of reading, with the best manuscripts almost equally divided; that is very unusual in our text of the New Testament. That is true, but I think you can explain it; it isn't hard to see the *sort* of thing that happened. I am an authority on St Matthew, because St Matthew had to be translated from Aramaic into Greek, and I know what it feels like, translating the Bible. You open your letters at breakfast, and find one from Burns and Oates to say that you have translated the same word by "wilderness" in one chapter and by "desert" three chapters before, and oughtn't you to stick to the same word? Well, the man who translated St Matthew into Greek had a lot of difficulties to contend with, but not Burns and Oates. He went straight ahead; he found, it may be, the same identical set of Aramaic words in chapter xix as in chapter v, but he wasn't going to be bothered to look back and see how he had translated them in chapter v; he went straight ahead and did a fresh translation, which happened to be slightly different. That's all right until it comes to the copying. Then you get one earnest fellow at Antioch, say, who copies Matthew xix. 9 exactly as he found it, and another earnest fellow, say, at Ravenna, with a Burns and Oates complex, who makes Matthew xix. 9 correspond exactly with Matthew v. 32. Which means that the Eastern text and the Western text differ ever afterwards.

I don't think it's good textual criticism to suppose that the same phrase, giving a loop-hole for divorce, could have crept in by *accident* in two separate passages of St Matthew. Was it foisted in by design? I don't think that's good Higher Criticism. There are very few copyists in real life who will falsify a document by adding to it; and those few will only do it if they have strong reason to. But *was* the Church of the second and third centuries lax about the remarriage of *divorcées*? Far from that, it had to fight like mad against the Montanists to justify the remarriage of widows. No, there may conceivably be a manuscript error, but you can't bet on it; we have got, somehow, to justify the text as it stands. How are we to do that? The common view taken by Catholic commentators has always been, that our Lord offers relief to the injured husband exactly as the Church does, not in the form of divorce but in the form of legal separation. What he said amounts to this; that if you find your wife has been behaving badly you may turn her out of doors, but only if you find she has been behaving badly. And even if you do turn her out of doors, you can't remarry and she can't remarry; that would be adultery

That is the classical treatment of the difficulty. But it doesn't satisfy everybody; it doesn't satisfy a lot of Catholics. Why, yes, they say, it *might* mean that; but why on earth did our Lord express himself in such an ambiguous way, just when the Pharisees were trying to extract damaging admissions from him, and there was every reason to be careful about his terms? Just when he was dealing with a subject which would affect the happiness of millions of Christian people? So there is a whole crop of alternative suggestions. Perhaps the most ingenious of them runs like this. Why is it that our Lord doesn't use the language of the divorce court? He doesn't talk about the husband getting rid of his wife for adultery; he calls it *porneia*, which can mean any kind of sexual irregularity. Is it possible that this word was used specially and contemptuously by the Jews about people who married within the forbidden degrees? It seems to be used like that by St Paul in the first epistle to the Corinthians. And that would explain a puzzle in the fifteenth chapter of the Acts. When the Apostles debated the question, Need Gentile converts adopt the law of Moses? they concluded, No; but with certain reservations. They were to abstain from what was sacrificed to idols, from blood-meat and meat which had been strangled, and from "fornication". Surely that last item comes in very oddly there! It becomes enormously simpler if you translate "and from marriage within the forbidden degrees". If that were so, the meaning might be the same in the present passage. "A man who puts away his wife (unless, of course, his marriage was invalid through consanguinity) and marries another, acts adulterously."

Will that wash? The obvious difficulty is to see how, at the time at which our Lord was speaking and among the people to whom our Lord was speaking, the question of marriage within the forbidden degrees can have been a live issue. It may have been, but we've no evidence of it. There was Herod, to be sure, and Herodias, but Herod's brother Philip was still alive; and so, for that matter, was Mrs. Herod. No, to get that explanation across, I think you have to combine it with the idea of a fault in the manuscripts. Quite naturally, as that reference in the Acts appears to indicate, the early Church would be much more particular about the forbidden degrees than the heathen were. If so, you would often get a convert who had married, as a heathen, within the forbidden degrees, and must now get rid of his wife as a condition of receiving baptism. Consequently, the Greek translator of St Matthew, conscious that he would be read by a Gentile public, might put in a footnote, twice over, to say, "Of course this doesn't apply to those forbidden-degree cases you are always getting." That *may* be the truth; but it is all frightfully speculative. I don't see that you can bank on it.

Then there's another thing. If you could be certain that the Western text was right in Matthew xix, and that our Lord used the same words on both occasions; if you could be certain that those words which I have rendered "setting aside the matter of unfaithfulness" really represented the Aramaic words our Lord used, then the difficulty once more disappears. Because he doesn't say, "*except* on the ground of unfaithfulness"; he says, "leaving the whole question of unfaithfulness on one side". I could have given you a whole conference on the meaning of the Greek word *parektos*. It doesn't mean "except"; it means "over and above", "not paying attention to". And our Lord will simply have been saying this: "If a man turns his wife out of doors—guilty wife or innocent wife, who cares? It doesn't make any difference—and marries another, he is an adulterer". But then, I'm pretty certain that the true text in chapter xix is not that. In chapter xix he is represented as saying, "If a man turns his wife out of doors not on a charge of unfaithfulness"; the two interpretations don't square. And who is to tell us which is the right one? Once more, we are left speculating.

No, when you've considered all those ingenious interpretations, I think you have to say this. Any one of them *may* be true; and any one of them is more likely than the alternative of supposing that the early Church was absolutely at sea about our Lord's teaching on marriage—that somebody got it all wrong, and nobody took the trouble to tell him so. But we ought always, in apologetics, to put the other man's case at its strongest, and then deal with it. So here. Granted that our Lord *did* say, "He who puts his wife away except on the ground of unfaithfulness, and marries another, makes an adulteress of her", what did he mean? What can he have meant? And how was it that some of those who listened to him thought he was forbidding the remarriage of divorced persons altogether?

I think you have to fall back on the commonly received explanation which I gave you some minutes ago; but I think, also, that you can afford to be a little more subtle in your presentation of it than the standard theologies are. I doubt if our Lord was making any conscious distinction in his mind between divorce and legal separation. It all turns on the force of the Hebrew word for "and". Hebrew seldom uses a subordinate clause; it prefers to co-ordinate. It says, "the man who puts away his wife and marries another", not meaning two processes but one; meaning "the man who puts away his wife *in order to marry another*"; in fact, the man who effects an exchange of wives. Our Lord is contemplating two possible situations leading to divorce; the injured husband who can no longer bear the sight of his guilty wife, and the unfaithful husband who has bestowed his affections elsewhere, so that he wants to be free to remarry. And it is with this latter situation that he deals. *The man who turns his innocent wife out of doors to gratify his lust for another woman is an adulterer,* the implication is, of course, that no parade of legal proceedings can make him any the less an adulterer. Or perhaps "makes her (the first wife) into an adulteress"—whatever that means. What, then, of the husband who has discovered that his wife is unfaithful? Our Lord is not talking about him; we are not told whether he may remarry later on or not; he does not come into the picture. We are only talking about the man who is out to effect an exchange of wives, aside from any question of guilt on the part of his present wife.

How, then, do we explain the discrepancy in words between St Matthew and his fellow evangelists? I should guess that our Lord, as I say, made this utterance on two separate occasions; and that he did so, once in the longer and once in the shorter form. It was preserved twice in some early collection of his sayings, once in the longer and once in the shorter form. St Matthew happened to pick on one, the longer, and used it in chapter v. Probably also in chapter xix, though here it is conceivable that his editors have played him false. St Mark chose the shorter form; and St Luke also adopted it, either because he found it in St Mark, or independently. But all that is a mere question of criticism. Both forms mean the same thing.

Meanwhile, what *was* our Lord's teaching about marriage? This. "I tell you that he who casts his eyes on a woman so as to lust after her has already committed adultery with her in his heart." That is, the dangerous moment in a dangerous intimacy is not the one we think; it is several moments earlier. "It is not what goes into his mouth that makes a man unclean; what makes a man unclean is what comes out of his mouth . . . his sins of murder, adultery, fornication." That is, it is we who shape our destinies, not they us. "If I have washed your feet, I who am the Master and the Lord, you in your turn ought to wash one another's feet." That is, you cannot stop giving, and continue to possess. If people would live by *that* part of our Lord's teaching, there would be no divorces, and no need for them.

23

The Resurrection of the Body

When you talk to a materialist about death, he will always tell you that, at death, the soul is snuffed out like a candle. That is not a very new or a very illuminating proposition; it has an old-fashioned ring about it, like most of the materialist propaganda. It would have been more up-to-date to talk about gas. But if we use gas as our metaphor, we are more likely to adopt the position of the pantheist. The pantheist thinks of *soul* as a homogeneous mass of stuff floating about in creation, rather like gas; when it comes out of a particular jet, and is lit, that is *a* soul; and when the tap is turned off, that particular soul ceases to have any individual existence, but the gas of which it was really formed does not cease to exist, it finds its way back into a kind of enormous gasometer, and can be used again to form a fresh soul, or jet, when it is required. Christian thought finds itself more at home if it becomes more up-to-date still, and derives its metaphor from electric light. This body which we share with the beasts is like the wire in an electric light bulb; it is something which canalizes, and expresses, that force or current which we call the soul. And if the switch is turned off, the wire, which is our body, loses all its usefulness and all its point, but the current, the soul, though shut off from it, has not ceased to exist; it is still there, ready to manifest itself in other forms. The question we have to consider here is whether, and in what sense, the piece of wire which will mediate, through all eternity, the activity of a human soul, shining in heaven or producing a nasty, lurid glow in hell, is *the same* as that piece of wire which we now call our body, has a genuine continuity of existence with it.

It's very easy to be misled by metaphors when we are talking about the relation between soul and body. We fall into a natural trap when we talk about the soul as an immortal spirit imprisoned within the body; or of the body as a garment which the soul casts aside at the moment of death. Those fine phrases assume that the soul, like the body, is material, and that the two things act on one another materially; which is untrue to fact. Even if we exercise our imaginations rather more adventurously, and say that the body is like a sponge, and the soul like the water which the sponge absorbs; so that death is merely the squeezing out of the sponge, which leaves the sponge still there and the water still there, we are the victims of our own metaphor. The fact is that the relation of soul and body is something quite unique in our experience; and very naturally so. Because in all experience it is the soul that does the experiencing, and what is experienced is the body, or the world of matter in relation to our body—as when a particular relation is set up between our body and a brick wall by our walking into it.

The Christian philosophy of life, which is a much more comprehensive affair than our modern philosophies of life, quarrels with all these inadequate metaphors because they all treat the connexion which exists between my body and my soul as if it were something merely accidental; as if my body was a trap into which my soul happens to have fallen, though it might equally well have been anybody else; just as a mousetrap happens to catch this particular mouse but it might just as well have been any other mouse. Or as if my body were a garment which my soul happens to be wearing, but it might just as well have been any other soul, like hiring a suit of clothes. Whereas if you believe in God's creation and in God's Providence, you have to think of my soul rather as something made to measure; this particular body is meant for

this particular soul. Which the theologians put into simple
language for us by saying that my body has an aptitudinality
for my particular soul, and *vice versa*. It always reminds me of
that silly story of the man who was found looking under the
table after dinner, and when the waiter asked if he'd lost
anything, he said, "Yes, my meringue"; and when the waiter
offered to give him another meringue off the side-board, he
said, "You fool, it's got my false teeth in it." Anybody's meringue will do, but not anybody's false teeth. And your body
is made for your soul; either is part of you; to be associated
together is their natural state—that is the point. That is part
of the reason why we dislike the idea of death; it is the
violent separation of two things that were made for one
another. It's quite true, soul and body can exist without one
another, and your soul will have to exist without any body to
support it or to be the expression of it for centuries, as likely
as not—all the time that elapses between your death and the
general resurrection. But that is an unnatural state of things,
due to the Fall. If Adam hadn't sinned, he would presumably
have passed, body and soul, from the earthly paradise into the
heavenly paradise, with no separation at all.

Well, as I say, that seems a more comprehensive view of
what soul means and what body means, than any of these
Oriental ideas or these modern ideas which represent the
body as a trap into which, goodness knows how, the soul has
fallen, or as a garment which, goodness knows why, the soul
is condemned to wear. That body and soul naturally belong
to one another, and are therefore destined at last to be re-
united, lest each should remain for ever incomplete—that
gives an intelligible view of the situation. But have we any
proof of it, or do we have to take it simply on the word of
the Church, as something which has been handed down to
us with the rest of the Christian revelation? Well, it would
not be very surprising if we had no evidence on the subject;
because the day of resurrection hasn't happened yet, and it is
hard to see how we could be given any direct evidence of

what it will be like when it does. But as a matter of fact we
have been given some account of what resurrection will be
like and what the resurrection body will be like, in the accounts which the gospels give us of what happened on Easter
Day. And what happened on Easter Day ought to be good
proof to us that the resurrection to which Christians look
forward is not merely a survival of the soul, it is a rehabilita-
tion of the body, and a re-joining of the body to the soul.
Otherwise, why should so much emphasis have been laid on
the empty tomb?

For us all, our Blessed Lady always excepted, the reunion of
body and soul is deferred until the day when this material
creation will have served its purpose and will be cast on the
scrap heap; something of it will be rescued, this body that was
ours. Can we infer, from the events which immediately followed the Resurrection, what our bodies will be like after the
last judgement? Yes and no. Our Lord's body during the forty
days between Easter and the Ascension was a resurrection
body; but its celestial qualities were held in abeyance, neutralized, so to speak, by a special decree of God's will. In order
that we might have full proof of its continuity with the body
which hung on the Cross, it was still artificially adapted to the
conditions of earth. The theologians enumerate four special
qualities of the risen body; impassibility, subtlety or the power
of penetrating other bodies, agility or the power of unim-
peded movement, and clarity, the shining of the heavenly
light through it. Our Lord, when he had risen, seems to have
moved as he would; he vanished from the sight of the disciples
at Emmaus. And barriers were no barriers to him; he passed
through closed doors. Yet it would appear that his body offered resistance to the touch; he even ate and drank with his
disciples. It is only a partial lifting of the veil, then, that is
supplied by the history of our Lord's last days on earth.

What we have to confess, after all, is that we are not
qualified to form any picture for ourselves of the conditions
under which our eternal life will be lived, and therefore we

cannot form the picture of a body adapted to the structure, acclimatized to the airs, of eternity. Our forefathers, with their cosy, geocentric ideas of existence, only had to think of hell as a large hole in the ground, and heaven as a large platform suspended in the sky. We have long been too conscious of our mental limitations to feel any certainty about our physical categories. What is matter? What even, in the last analysis, is space? If you read Dante, you find you are expected to think of hell as a sort of enlarged edition of the Albert Hall, and heaven as constructed roughly on the same principles as a wedding-cake. All that facility for eternity-building has left us; we are content to feel that when we get there we shall know what it is like. And we are therefore all the more grateful for St Paul's assurances in the first epistle to the Corinthians—St Paul, who lived so long before Galileo, so long before Einstein—that there are bodies terrestrial and bodies celestial; that the glory of the terrestrial is one, and the glory of the celestial another; that the difference between a blade of wheat fully grown, and the shrivelled seed you dropped in the ground months before, is only a faint indication of the difference between our bodies, as we know them here on earth, and our bodies, as they will be in heaven.

But, you say, they will be the same bodies; that was part of what we set out to establish. Yes, the same bodies, but expressing themselves, surely, in different terms. It is the same unit of electricity which can take the form of a flash of light, or a glow of heat, or a tickling sensation in your hand; the same thing, expressing itself in different terms. Identity can persist without similarity; and therefore I never could get up much enthusiasm about those speculations which some theologians indulge in over the exact details of a heavenly existence; telling us that we shall look the same as we do here, and at the same time be perfectly beautiful—which will be hard work for some of us—or that we shall all be exactly thirty-three. I am content to think of my present body as merely the inadequate symbol of that body which will be mine in eternity.

A symbol, yes; but we must remind ourselves again, it isn't merely a kind of book token, entitling me to the possession of *a* body in eternity; it is rather a kind of cloakroom ticket, entitling me to the possession of *my* body in eternity. Our Lord's Resurrection meant an empty tomb; our Lord's Ascension meant, presumably, the disappearance from earth of a certain quantum of matter which had previously been part of earth. If it is going to be possible to establish identity between that body of yours which will lie in Kensal Green, and that body of yours which will, we hope, attain the enjoyment of heaven, aren't we going to land ourselves in rather difficult physical speculations to account for it?

The critics of our religion, as most of us know, have made merry over these difficulties from the earliest times. The favourite objection used to be that if a man was eaten by cannibals, there would be certain particles of matter which would belong both to the cannibal and to the victim of the experiment. And it has often been pointed out that, even in civilized countries, we may find ourselves eating mutton that comes from a sheep which has been browsing in the church-yard, and so the same difficulty arises in a rather more circui-tous way. And, while arguments like these have suggested to irreverent minds the possibility that there will not be enough bodies to go round, so to speak, on the day of judgement, it is equally easy to suggest that there will be too many bodies going about; because after all you and I change, even in the course of a single year, nearly all the material particles which go to make up our bodies, so that it would be very hard to know which of a series of material bodies we are going to rise with. Sceptical difficulties like these have led some Catholic thinkers to suggest—and I understand that it is an allowable position—that the identity between the earthly and the heavenly body is formal, rather than material; depends upon the persistence, not of actual material particles, but of

the form which organized them. The trouble about that is
that if you are a good Thomist—if you are a Scotist, I fancy
you get out of it, somehow—you hold that the form which
organizes our material bodies is nothing other than the soul;
a dead body has a different form from a living body, something which is called a *forma cadaverica*. And if so, you see,
asserting the resurrection of the body would be no more
than asserting the resurrection of the soul, and it is difficult to
see how or why the reembodied soul in heaven differs from
the disembodied soul in Purgatory.

For this reason, the more cautious among Catholic authors
are content to point out that we needn't insist on the necessity
of reassembling every individual particle of the terrestrial body
in heaven. Part will do: and, precisely in view of the large
number of transformations which our body has been through,
it ought to be possible to make good any losses through canni-
balism. I confess that I find it a little difficult to frame my mind
with confidence into this particular type of orthodoxy. I
should prefer to think that, without meddling with any controversies between Thomists and Scotists, we can take refuge
here in our ignorance. Within the limited circle of our physical experience, we have to take matter, at least for common-
sense purposes, as an ultimate category which cannot be
further defined or explained. But we all feel that there must be
a further explanation at the back of it, which an experience
wider than our earthly experience would give us; that the
distinction between form and matter, however sound it may
be for our present purposes, does not exhaust the truth which
it proposes to us; and therefore, that there may be such a thing
as physical, not merely spiritual identity, which nevertheless
cannot be stated in terms of matter as we know it. What is
certain is that the thing, whatever it is, which expresses itself
here and now in terms of a mass of matter about six feet high,
will persist, although it may be expressed in quite different
terms, in that order of creation, whatever it be, which will
succeed when the material creation itself has passed away.

The practical importance of that truth for us is, I take it, that as Christians we are bound to think of our bodies as part of ourselves, as included not only in the scheme of our creation but in the scheme of our redemption, as having, therefore, a supernatural importance, and as demanding reverence in our treatment of them. We look forward, as St Paul says, to the redemption of our bodies; they are not encumbrances which we drag about with us, they are first-fruits of eternity, entrusted to our keeping. Christian thought, if you will look deep enough, is always turning out to be the *via media* between two opposing forms of error. If you lean towards Eastern spiritualism, you will find yourself talking, like the man in that poem of Lyall's, about your body as if it were something that didn't matter; it "is a garment no more fitting, is a tent that I am quitting, is a snare, from which at last, like a hawk, my soul hath passed". If you lean towards Western materialism, you will find yourself talking about your body as if it were the only thing that mattered, like that poem of Housman's, "The Immortal Part", which ends up "And leave with endless night alone the steadfast and enduring bone". If you avoid both those excesses, you will find yourself talking like Thomas à Kempis:

> Ah, frail body, earth forsaking,
>> In what glory wilt thou rise,
> Passing fair in thy remaking,
>> Strong and whole and swift and wise,
> Free, and joy in freedom taking,
>> Framed for life that never dies!
> Up, and stir thee, onward spur thee;
>> What, though toil be hard to bear,
> If God's grace shall count thee worthy
>> Those unguessed rewards to share?
> Brief the pains that shall prefer thee
>> To eternal glory there.